The Evolution Of Religion
An Anthropological Study

by

L. R. Farnell

ABOUT THE AUTHOR

Lewis Richard Farnell FBA was an Oxford professor who studied ancient literature and was Vice-Chancellor from 1920 to 1923. He was born in 1856 and died in 1934. Lewis Farnell was born in 1856 in Salisbury, which is in the south of England. He went to school at the City of London School and Exeter College, Oxford. In 1878, he got a first class degree in Literae Humaniores from Exeter College. It was 1880 when he was made a Fellow of Exeter College and 1883 when he was made a lecturer in classics. His next job was as Rector, or head, of the College. Farnell took a number of trips around Europe between 1880 and 1893. He studied ancient archaeology in Berlin and Munich and also visited Asia Minor and Greece. He was an associated member of the German Archaeological Institute starting in 1901. In June of that year, he got his D.Litt. from the University of Oxford. Farnell became a Fellow of the British Academy in 1916. Besides that, the universities of Dublin (Ireland), St. Andrews (Scotland), and Geneva (Switzerland) gave him honors degrees.

CONTENTS

Preface

A small book on a great and difficult subject must explain and apologise for itself, especially if it cannot claim a *raison d'être* as a handbook for beginners. Having accepted the stimulating invitation to give in the spring of this year a short series of lectures for the Hibbert Trust on some subject belonging to the department of comparative religion, I felt that it was desirable to avoid those topics that had been appropriated by former lecturers; and also that the Trustees, as well as the audience, deserved that what the lecturer put forth should embody the results of some personal and original study. I finally selected for special discussion the ritual of purification, and the influence of the ideas associated with it upon law, morality, and religion; and secondly, the development of prayer from lower to higher forms. These subjects do not appear to have been as yet exhaustively treated by modern anthropology or scientific and comparative theology, and I had already worked upon them to some extent as "parerga" of the treatise that I am completing for the Clarendon Press on the history of Greek cults. I am aware that these special questions would well repay longer and more minute research, and could each furnish material for a large volume. But having been advised to publish the lectures more or less as they were delivered, I put them forth as tentative and incomplete work. I specially regret to have been unable to have gone further at present into the Egyptian evidence, with the kindly proffered assistance of Mr Griffiths, the Reader in Egyptology at Oxford.

The first two lectures, dealing with the methods and the value of the study of comparative religion and its relations to anthropology, are of a more general character. If they seem to occupy somewhat too large a part of a work of this small compass, the urgency of the questions they raise may serve as an apology. It was suggested to me that some such pronouncement might be timely at the point we have reached. For the subject is winning greater consideration, and even receiving endowment, in the organisation of the newer Universities. From the scientific point of view it is one of the most fascinating of studies; and its practical importance for our colonial administrators and our missionaries is obvious to those who reflect. It is also a legitimate hope that its wider and more intelligent recognition in England may tend to cool and temper the heated atmosphere of dogmatic controversy, by presenting religious facts in their true proportion and proper setting.

I must take this opportunity of expressing my gratitude to many friends for valuable assistance, and especially to my friend and colleague, Mr R. Marett, to whose comprehensive knowledge of the religious thought and ritual of savage races I owe many important clues.

L. R. FARNELL.

August, 1905.

LECTURES I AND II
THE COMPARATIVE STUDY OF RELIGIONS:
ITS METHOD AND PROBLEMS

The reasonable and sympathetic study of the various religions of mankind, which are perhaps the clearest mirror we possess of human feeling, aspiration, and thought in its highest and lowest forms, is only possible for the individual or for the age that feels no constraining call to suppress and obliterate all save one cherished creed. Such study began, as we should expect, in the earlier Hellenic period, the Hellenic religion throwing few or no obstacles in the way of undogmatic investigation; and the first anthropologist of religion is Herodotus. Then among Hellenistic scholars and those of pre-Christian Rome there were some who devoted themselves to the collection and exposition of the religious institutions of foreign races. But save a few short treatises, such as Plutarch's *De Iside et Osiride*, Sallustius' *De Diis et Mundo*, Lucian's *De Dea Syria*, nothing has survived beyond the titles and the fragments of their works; and by an irony of fortune we owe much of our knowledge of Hellenic and other religions of the Mediterranean area to the Christian controversialists, who reveal many of the essential features of the various pagan creeds in order to expose them to obloquy: they could not anticipate that we should gather as the fruit of their labours a better appreciation than we could otherwise have gained of the religions which they strove to destroy, and possibly of Christianity itself. If I were attempting, as I do not propose to attempt, to give a complete survey of the growth and development of the study which we are considering, I should probably be able to cull but little material for the narrative from Byzantine and mediæval sources. We may note that the spirit of these ages was, on the whole, alien to our present interest; and that it is not till after the Renaissance and the discovery of America that systematic work in this field begins again. To two Spaniards of Peruvian and Mexican descent,3.1 we owe our knowledge of the religions of the Incas and the Aztecs, that of the latter at least being of prime importance for the student of the higher religions of mankind. A Polish nobleman of the 16th century has left us a fairly detailed account of the religious practices and beliefs of the then semi-pagan Lithuania.3.2 But it may be regarded as one of the greatest achievements of the latter part of the 19th century to have raised the comparative study of religion to a high position in the whole domain of inductive speculation and inquiry. And its development has been mainly due to two independent lines of investigation. The first stimulus came with the discovery and the interpretation of the sacred books of the East, a momentous epoch in the history of European thought, and certain important theories concerning religious origins were put forth by Vedic scholars, and based on the evidence of Vedic literature: at the same time the decipherment of the Assyrian-Babylonian and Egyptian texts has contributed a wealth of new material, and has started new problems of religious inquiry, which specially concern the students of Hellenic as well as those of Semitic antiquity. But an equally or, as some may think, more powerful factor in the recent advance towards the organised knowledge of religions has been the growth, in the last half-century, of the study that has appropriated the name of anthropology, which is generally understood to mean the study of primitive or savage man, both in the past and the present, in respect of his physical and mental conditions. It is quite unnecessary for me to dilate on the high and manifold utility, both practical and speculative, of this new branch of human inquiry; the theme has become almost a popular commonplace in the leading journalism of the day. And anthropology, defined as above, has a definite value and object apart from its contributions to our knowledge of the religions of the world. It is nevertheless true that the religious interest in England is so strong and penetrating, that many of our leading anthropologists, in their investigations of savage society, have directed their attention mainly to religious or quasi-religious phenomena. Even if their labours were confined to the discovery and the exposition of savage ritual and belief, we should still be greatly indebted to them; for to many of us at least the savage man is interesting in his own right, whether it is true or not that the study of his mental phenomena helps to explain the mental phenomena of our higher selves or of the higher races in the past. But these writers claim, and I think with right, to have done more than this, and by comparison, induction, and hypothesis to have thrown some light on the evolution of religion from lower to higher forms, and therefore to have laid the foundation for the science with which we are concerned. Also attempts have been recently made by an accomplished scholar of the new doctrine, Dr Frazer, to trace what may be called the anthropological genesis of the central idea of Christianity itself.6.1 It is not then surprising that in England at least such claims and such ambitions should excite mistrust, even hostility, and the prestige of anthropology may have also suffered at times from the indiscretion of its friends. Still, its work is of wide vogue, its energy exuberant, and its influence in the future assured. In considering, therefore, the aims and methods of the comparative science of religion, it has appeared to me that its relations to anthropology are now one of the main points in the inquiry. And we may seem to have reached a stage where it is desirable to test our position, to take stock as it were, to examine our methods, and to consider whether they are capable of improvement. The task is difficult, and in facing it one must face the imputation of presumption, especially as in a short course of lectures one must be brief, and may therefore appear over-dogmatic.

If the comparative study of religion is to examine, as on the ground of its title it must, the various recorded or discoverable religions of every branch of the human family, then a part of anthropology, limited, as it has usually chosen to limit itself, to the study of the savage races, is obviously a sub-department of the whole. And its work, conducted often under great difficulties, has been solid, well-organised, and of high importance. Even those who deny its claim to be called a science, whatever that word may mean, must admit that it is at least an indispensable branch of historic inquiry, and that it has deepened the self-knowledge of mankind.

Some of its pioneers may have been overeager in their theorising, premature in their attempts to reveal the origin of all religion in some savage ritual or in the background of savage thought, for instance in ancestor-worship or totemism. Such rash generalisations are inevitable in the opening periods of a new study, and may be discredited or abandoned without discrediting the investigations that gave rise to them. We may have come to be aware of the excesses of the students of totemism: we may have come to the conviction that neither theirs nor any other special and single hypothesis has as yet supplied us with the master-clue by which we can penetrate to the aboriginal source of human religion: we may have found scientific reasons for rejecting the belief that all gods arose as ghosts of departed ancestors. But if we discard such theories of origin, we owe this negative result to the maturer study of anthropology itself; and we may owe to it the positive induction that the religious product at the different stages and in the different branches of mankind was a complex growth from many different germs.

It has taught us also much more than this. It has shown us that all through the present societies of savage men there prevails an extraordinary uniformity, in spite of much local variation, in ritual and mythology, a uniformity so striking as to suggest belief in an ultimately identical tradition, or, perhaps more reasonably, the psychologic theory that the human brain-cell in different races at the same stage of development responds with the same religious speech or the same religious act to the same stimuli supplied by its environment.

We have learnt to discover a certain savage style, as we may call it, in myth and ritual; and anthropology has performed a twofold work of comparison; for it has not only compared the various savage races of mankind, but it has compared the results of this colligation with the religious phenomena of the higher races, and has revealed the savage style in much of their mythology and ritual. It was first discovered by the earlier investigators of the antiquity of Northern Europe, such as the brothers Grimm and Mannhardt, that underlying the religion of Christendom lay a stratum of peasant-ritual and belief, not yet extinct nor likely soon to be, that reveals the same mental condition in early Europe that exists among our savage contemporaries in various parts of the world. Then the sacred edifice of Hellenism was attacked; and the complacency of Hellenic scholars was sometimes disturbed by the revelation, through a strict comparative method, of the same savage style in much of Hellenic ritual and Hellenic myth. Thus for the first time we came to understand the true significance of many of the crude and repulsive facts in Hellenic religion—the human sacrifices, the reverence paid to animals, stones, and trees, the demonology and magic rites. Many of these practices had lost their meaning for the more advanced generations, who nevertheless retained them under the strong constraint of religious conservatism; but if we find the same practices among existing races who perform them with a living and plenary faith as part of a quasi-logical structure of belief, we can place them back into their proper setting when we discover them still surviving in the higher and alien society. Greek religion especially, having never violently broken with its own past, is a bed of rich deposit still inviting exploration. And now Hellenic scholars are ransacking the same treasure for further anthropological material; while Assyriologists and Egyptologists are treating a part of the phenomena of their special departments in the same spirit.

We realise the gain of this: we are slowly and surely arriving at inductive conclusions concerning the similarity of development through which the higher and lower races have passed and are passing; the solidarity of the human family appears stronger than we might have supposed. At the same time we have now to be on our guard against certain common anthropological fallacies. Some of these are less inevitable than others: for instance, that which we may call the fallacy of simple enumeration. On the ground of the general inductive belief that the higher races have at one time passed through a savage phase, it is often too rashly assumed that each and all of them must at one time have possessed a particular institution, such as totemism or ancestor-worship, which, as a matter of fact, is found among the majority of the savage races of to-day. This is to exaggerate the principle of solidarity, to ignore the fact of the great diversity actually observable among existing primitive societies, and the possibility that it was just by avoiding some particular detrimental institution that some of the higher peoples were able to proceed on their path of progress. Again, the anthropological explanation is often obliged to be hypothetical, for the evidence presented is often very fragmentary: by means of a reasonable and expert imagination, an attempt is made to reconstruct a whole fabric out of a few fragments. A single bone may enable the expert biologist to reshape unerringly the once living animal; but in anthropology the fragment in question may have descended from either one of two differing organisms or organic institutions that may have left very much the same imprint upon mythology and religion. For instance, a full-fledged totemistic system, having fallen into decay, might leave its trace in certain stories about animals or in occasional reverence paid to a particular animal: but direct animal-worship, a religious view that may be quite independent of totemism, or certain forms of ancestor-worship may equally well have deposited the same fossil-thought or fossil-rite.13.1 And we know how recklessly the theory of the ubiquitous practice of human sacrifice has been used to explain certain peculiar phenomena in later ritual, such as the scourging of the Spartan boys, for example.

But a stricter anthropology can correct the over-narrow hypotheses of its immaturity, and can render masterly aid to the evolutionary study of the higher religions; for each of these, in spite of revelation or transforming enthusiasm that would obliterate the past, contains a mass of mysterious dead matter; and it is for the anthropologist to show the prior functional organic significance of this. But if, in obedience to the currently accepted limitation of his subject, he confines himself mainly to the study of savage life and to the dead matter of the higher religions, and yet is tempted to deal with the more vital and essential elements in these, he will be liable to the special bias of his own study. We may note such bias in recent attempts to explain the essential features of the Eleusinian Mysteries in the light of merely savage anthropology. And of course we are all apt to lose the sense of proportion and to exaggerate the importance of the special phenomena to which we confine our regard. The folk-lorist will be liable to over-emphasise the part played by mythology in religion, and may ignore the higher importance of prayer and ritual; for the most conscientious cobbler is never really able to stick to his last. In fact, though the whole exposition of the higher religions is impossible without anthropology, there is some danger at present lest the part be at times mistaken for the whole. For instance, we may feel with some uneasiness that recent expositions of Hellenic religion tend, unintentionally no doubt, to distort the view of the reader and to produce a false impression by exaggerating the savage and primitive facts, missing the true perspective and misjudging the whole. Our appreciation of Greek mythology may suffer in the same way, unless we can keep the keen edge of our appreciative faculty: the Greek myth has often its striking affinities with the Arunta or the Pawnee, and it is necessary for comparative folk-lore and anthropology to point this out, and often to insist on the beauty of the legend and the dignity of the religious thought among savages: but it is unfortunate if these studies should result in our loss of the perception that Greek mythology, after all, is the most beautiful of any of which we have record.

The fallacy which I have so far tried to indicate arises from the temper of mind that a special study is liable to engender. On the other hand, there is a particular fallacy of method to which the modern study of anthropology, as it has chosen to limit itself, specially exposes us. It is liable to withdraw us from the immediate entourage of a particular fact—a particular legend or a religious service—to the distant circumference. It was inevitable for the earliest pioneers of the study to travel far, for the circumference was unexplored, and there were facts lying at the distant points that concerned us. But, after all, our first object of study should be the more immediate environment of the thing which we wish to understand. The student of Hellenic religion and myth may have ultimately to roam, in a literary sense, into Central Australia and the byways of America; but he ought first to explore the Mediterranean regions and the lands of anterior Asia. It is interesting, and may be necessary, to know "the Pawnee version of the Eleusinia"; but, for the true understanding of the great Greek mystery, certain elements in the Egyptian religion, in Mithraism, and in Christianity itself will probably afford a more illuminative comparison. The mind of our student is sometimes tempted, in fact, to travel too easily and too cheaply to the other side of the globe, and to leave undone work that should first have been done nearer home.

To reduce these ideas to something like a working formula of method, may we say that the anthropology which the comparative study of any one of the more complex and advanced religions immediately demands is "an adjacent anthropology"? For religious ideas, legends, and ritual are most contagious, and tend to propagate themselves over large contiguous areas: for, to reverse a stereotyped question, "what is less its own than a people's gods?" We greatly desiderate an anthropology of the Mediterranean basin, including anterior Asia; for there are strong reasons for the belief that from very early times the frequent intercourse of the leading peoples in this region endowed them with a common stock of religious ideas, ritual, and legend which have probably left their impress on the higher religions of the world. It is these that specially interest most of us, and we feel we cannot solve their problems by means of savage anthropology alone. Why, after all, should the latter term be restricted, as it usually is, to the study of savage life? Doubtless we cannot so extend the use of the word as to cover its full etymological signification: else it would come to include the whole of human history from the beginning down to the present, and would lose its value as a mark of any special science. But we might somewhat enlarge its present connotation with advantage to the comparative method, and without a too wide departure from current usage. We might define the anthropological study of any one of the higher religions as an evolutionary study of its embryology: the evolutionary law might appear in the first instance as a proximate law of growth. For probably every one of the world-creeds has inherited, apart from its own achievement, a double tradition, a tradition from the more remote and one from the more immediate past. The first may descend from immemorial antiquity, and from really primitive or savage mental and social life; and it has been the task of primitive anthropology to expound and explain the facts that this tradition has deposited. But many if not most of these facts may be regarded as functionally dead matter surviving in the more advanced system of belief, and as not belonging to its essential life. On the other hand, from the immediate tradition much will be found to have been taken over by an inevitable law of assimilation, certain potent ideas which, though transformed, will enter into the very life-blood of the new creed. And these are to be discovered and analysed by what I have ventured to call an "adjacent" anthropology, which will include a comprehensive study of the literature and monuments belonging to the more proximate past of the race which develops the new faith as well as of the races that are its nearer neighbours.

Such a method, though not hitherto styled anthropological, has already been applied by various scholars in the different parts of our field; the exposition of the Babylonian elements in Judaic religion, of the Judaic and pagan elements in Moslemism, are examples of it. On the present occasion I would prefer to illustrate it by noting its application to the scientific study of Christianity itself, of which the remarkable complexity, the variety of forms that it has assumed in different parts of Christendom at different periods, seems specially to invite the higher anthropological treatment. Moreover it probably contains a richer deposit than any other of the world-religions from the various streams of thought and belief that nourished the life of early civilised or semi-civilised man. The illustration drawn from our own religion will be also more personally interesting to ourselves; and though the limits of time and my own knowledge may prevent me from putting forth any original statement, yet something may be gained and a more extended interest awakened by a brief notice of what has been and what remains to be done.

There is now no need for apology if one wishes frankly to consider the genesis of the fundamental ideas and prevailing institutions of earlier and later Christianity, although hitherto a certain religious shyness, which belongs to the national character, may have made English scholars reluctant to attempt the anthropology of our national faith; and the progress of the subject owes more to foreign workers. Our own theological students of distinction have not evaded the question as to the early influences that may have moulded the religious thought of Christ and St Paul; but these were naturally sought mainly in the later Judaism; and though the debt of the developed Christianity to Hellenic philosophy has never been ignored, yet that neither our sacred books nor Judaic literature nor Greek philosophy explain the whole complex of historic Christianity, is a conviction of recent growth, and the investigations to which it has prompted are recent. For instance, it was a new departure of great promise for the future of our science when, in a course of Hibbert lectures delivered some years ago, Dr Hatch publicly expounded the deep indebtedness of Christianity in respect of ritual, organisation, and even religious concept to the Eleusinian Mysteries and other mystic societies of Greek lands. And the few students of Hellenic religion in England have often noted its many ties of affinity with our own, though of these there has been as yet no complete and authoritative account. We may admit that the triumph of a new and great creed may imply a potent revelation, perhaps a sudden mental transformation in the catechumens difficult to equate with any formulated law of evolution. Still we cannot gainsay the experience that as the religion establishes and organises itself, it draws nourishment from the old soil which is full of the living germs of past organisms. Therefore it was inevitable that Hellenic religion should leave a deep impress upon earlier and later Christianity; partly because the religious temper in the Greek world throughout the centuries immediately preceding the adoption of Christianity was more powerful and fervid than it had been in the days of Homer or Pericles, and mainly because Hellenic converts became the pillars of the Church. But the comparative student must pursue the problem further afield and beyond the track of Hellas. The old Phrygian religion, which Professor Ramsay's travels and investigations have assisted us to know, must be seriously taken into account; for Phrygia was one of the earliest homes of Christianity, its aboriginal religion had germinated in ideas strikingly akin to some that are primary in all or many of the creeds of Christendom; and the morbid and ecstatic temperament of the native Phrygian, which gave so distinct a colour to the Cybele-Attis cult, seems to have appeared again in certain schismatic forms of Christian doctrine in Phrygia, especially in the heresy of Montanism. Finally, we may learn much, even adopt much, from our enemies. The most dangerous antagonists of Christianity were, after all, the worship of Isis and Mithraism. It may be possible to trace the influence of these on their conqueror: the great work of M. Cumont on Mithras cult suggests at least many interesting religious parallels; and even the older Zoroastrian literature must be considered within the range of necessary and legitimate comparison.

As I am here concerned with illustration of method rather than with positive proof, I can only offer a very brief summary of the results which the anthropological study of Christianity has hitherto achieved, and may yet achieve.

The religious affinities discoverable between the earlier and later "Mediterranean" systems may be classified according as they appear in the legends, in nomenclature and terminology, in external symbols and liturgical objects, in hieratic institutions, and finally in the ideas, aspirations, and concepts of faith. As regards legend and mythology, a great historic religion may of course claim to be free from all mythology; nevertheless it is a matter of experience that popular legends are sure at some period earlier or later to creep in, for the people insist on telling the old stories under changed names. I myself have heard the immemorial story of Odysseus walking inland with his oar, which the rustic mistakes for a winnowing-fan, told about St Peter, St Paul, and St John on the coast of the Peloponnese; just as an old Norse legend about Odin and Baldur is retold of Christ and St Peter.26.1 And students of mediæval hagiology will discover more and more clearly various fragments of pre-Christian mythology embedded in the legends of the saints. Such facts are the material of comparative folk-lore, which plays a useful but quite subordinate part in the work of comparative religion. Legends have indeed their own independent interest, poetical, ethical, and other; but the importance of mere mythology in the study of religion has been often much overrated; St Augustine, mistaking Greek legends for Greek religion, could discover no morality in it at all,26.2 and modern scholars have inherited the fallacy. Myths are often irresponsible, capricious, volatile, and flit like a vapour round the solid structure of real belief and ritual. A high religion may attract low myths: some of our own are not spotless, but Christianity can ignore them. The myth that is an essential fact for the student of religion is that which enshrines some living religious idea or institution, or one which proves the survival of some ritual or faith that belonged to an older system. I may note a few of this kind which illustrate the affinities of Judaic, Christian, and pagan legend. The cessation of human-sacrifice in the Mediterranean area, the awakening of the conviction that the practice was abhorrent to a merciful God, implied so momentous a change in religious and moral thought and practice that it would be strange if it left no legendary record of itself. We may discern one in the story of Abraham's sacrifice; to which we find a very striking and close parallel in the Laconian legend of Helen, whose father intended to sacrifice her to God in order to stay a plague:27.1 the eagle, the messenger of God, swooped down and snatched the knife from the sacrificer's hand, and let it fall on a kid that was pasturing near. Again, we are all familiar with the story of Jephtha's vow: the fact is not so well known that a story identical in nearly every detail was told of Idomeneus, the Cretan hero,28.1 who vowed that if he returned home from the Trojan war he would sacrifice to God the first thing that he met on landing: his daughter was the first that met him—and Idomeneus "did with her according to his vow," or intended to do so, and the people exiled him for it. Different from these, but belonging to the inner circle, so to speak, of sacred narrative, are one or two Gospel stories which are not peculiar to Palestine or to our sacred books. The miraculous star that guides sacred personages on a divine errand must be an Anatolian star-legend, for it is told of Æneas and his voyage to Italy.28.2 And a critical appreciation of the style of Hellenic folk-lore detects at once a marked Hellenic colour in the legends that gather around the birth and rearing of the Virgin in the apocryphal Gospel of St James. More important and suggestive of much more is the parallelism that we discover between the story of our Lord's temptation and the temptation of Zarathustra in the Zend-Avesta: here also the evil god offers the holy prophet the kingdoms of the world if he will fall down and worship him.29.1

Finally, it is not improbable that the strange legend preserved in various late Greek MSS., of the Virgin Mary's descent into hell,29.2 where she is shown the torments of the damned, is derived ultimately from the Babylonian myth of the descent of Ischtar, which in the Greek world transformed itself into the story of the descent of Aphrodite. This suggestion is in harmony with the evidence which will be noticed below for the belief that the development of the worship and the divine character of the Virgin owed much, directly or indirectly, to the great Anatolian cult of the mother-goddess.

As regards the legend just mentioned, we may suppose direct borrowing, or at least direct mental suggestion from an older mythology and faith. To the other examples which I have adduced—probably only a few among many that might be quoted—the theory of borrowing may be inappropriate.

It may be more scientific, and certainly it is at present more expedient, to be content with the assumption that for thousands of years over contiguous human areas a similarity of religious temperament, religious institutions, religious crises may tend to produce a common stock of legend; whether the legend is true or false is not our present concern.

I turn now to the second group of affinities, those in nomenclature and terminology. This may at first sight appear a matter unimportant for the evolution of religion, and of merely linguistic concern. A people changing its religion cannot suddenly change its speech, but must adapt the old terminology to the new thought. It may be of interest for the student of language to know that when St Paul promises to "show you a mystery" he is borrowing the language of paganism; that when Bishop Clemens31.1 ecstatically exclaims, "The Lord is our hierophant; bearing the sacred torch He has marked the initiate with His own seal... once join our mystery and you will dance in the choir of angels," he is using the phraseology of the Eleusinian and Attis Mysteries. But the interest of such a style, upon which Dr Hatch has sufficiently commented, is more than linguistic; for it foreshadows a real though fortunately a temporary change which came over Christianity in the first few centuries of its life, transforming it from an open doctrine into a mystery organised after the old Greek type. Moreover the modern logical view of names as merely indifferent speech-symbols, which can be changed without affecting the essence of the things, was by no means the old-world view. The formula *nomina sunt numina* was valid in all the old religions of the Mediterranean area, including earlier and even later Christianity: the divine name was felt to be part of the divine essence and itself of supernatural potency; and this will be seen to be of paramount importance when we consider the forms of ancient prayer. Therefore the propagation of a new religion was greatly assisted if it could allow itself to employ some at least of the names potent and familiar in the older creed. Now the personal names of the various deities of paganism, owing to the mental illusion noted above, were necessarily hateful to the new faith and were ruthlessly suppressed, surviving merely as names of demons or for purposes of magic: only in remote corners of the old world one or two may still be lingering, purified as it were and at peace, as in the modern chapel of "Panagia Aphroditissa," near the old Paphos in Cyprus. But some of the sacred names of Greek paganism were mere appellatives, possessing less individual personality, and were therefore innocent in the ears of the Christian propagandists. And two of these were destined to become names of primary virtue in the terminology of the new faith. When the apostles and their successors preached the Gospel of "the Saviour," this title could awaken at least a responsive religious thrill in the hearts of the Hellenes who had been nursed in their ancestral religion. For it had long been attached to their supreme god, and in its feminine form to their beloved goddess Kore, and as applied to her the appellative already connoted "salvation" after death;33.1 and already it had been used by the Alexandrian Greeks to sanctify the divine man, God's representative on earth, "the living image of God," as one of the later Ptolemies is styled in the ecstatic language of the

Rosetta inscription.34.1 But in the history of divine names none have been of greater import for paganism and Christianity alike than "Kore-Parthenos" and that of the Greek and Phrygian "Divine Mother," the Θεῶν Μήτηρ. It is at least probable that the prevalence of the cult and the name of "Kore," the goddess who proffered salvation in the pre-Christian Hellenic world, afforded strong stimulus to the later growth and diffusion of Mariolatry, which is one of those phenomena in the history of the Church which cannot be adequately explained without looking beyond the limits of Christianity proper. A passage in the Panarium of Epiphanios34.2 is of singular interest for those who wish to study the period of transition between old things and new. This writer tells us that on the night of the 5th or 6th of January, in Alexandria, the worshippers met in the sacred enclosure or temple of "Kore," and having sung hymns to the music of the flute till dawn, they descended by the light of torches into an underground shrine and brought up thence a wooden idol on a bier representing Kore, seated and naked, with the sign of the cross on her brow, her hands, and her knees. And with the accompaniment of flutes, hymns, and dances the image was carried round the central shrine seven times, before it was restored again to its nether dwelling-place: "and the votaries say that to-day at this hour Kore—that is, the Virgin—gave birth to the Eternal."

It is strange that Epiphanios should quote this rite as an example of pure paganism. This cannot be true: the image has been carefully signed with the cross in such a way as to suggest, not casual violence, but the deliberate intention of the worshippers; nor could the formula, "the Virgin has born the Eternal," have been part of a purely pagan liturgy consecrated to the Hellenic Kore. Still less could the service be purely Christian: at least I imagine that a naked Virgin, kept in a cavern shrine and carried round with timbrels, would be a unique fact in Christian archæology. The belief is forced upon us that we have here a blending of at least two rival creeds in a period of transition. An old ritual of Kore at Alexandria, the goddess of the underworld whose statue was kept in a subterraneous cavern, may have included a kind of passion play in which a holy child was born: as this occurred near the beginning of January, it could all the more easily be adapted to the requirements of a gradually prevailing Christianity. The idol is sanctified with the sign of the cross, and the child is called "the Aion." This name betrays the influence at work. The doctrine which laboured most zealously to combine the various elements of the pagan and Christian creeds was Gnosticism, and "Aion" was a figure which the Gnostics borrowed from Mithraism.37.1 It seems that the religious rays from Hellas, Persia, and Bethlehem converged at the "Korion" of Alexandria. But the name Κόρη does not seem to have usually formed part of the sacred title accepted by the early Church for the Mother of our Lord. Probably the name had acquired a personal association with the pagan goddess too strong to allow it to be used for the new faith;37.2 nor was the idea of virginity so directly connoted by it as by the term παρθένος: hence ἡ ἁγνὴ παρθένος or ἡ ἁγία παρθένος is chosen for the Christian appellation of Mary. But these words themselves belong to the ancient hieratic vocabulary of Hellas, for the maiden-goddess known by no other name than Parthenos had long been adored in various states of Asia Minor and Thrace;38.1 "Hagne," the "Holy One," was a divinity dear to the Arcadians;38.2 and at Assos, the chief port of Mysia, visited by St Paul on one of his journeys, an inscription attests that "the Holy Virgin of our fatherland"—such is her style—had been pre-eminent in the pagan worship.38.3 Moreover the sacred title, "the Mother of God," was sympathetic with a very ancient and dominant Mediterranean faith: in prehistoric times from Crete, and at a later period from Phrygia, had gone forth the worship of the divine mother, known generally as "the Gods' Mother" or "the Mother," which had left a deep impress upon the religious imagination of the various races of the Greek and Roman world. It is no paradox to affirm that one of the streams that fostered the later growth of Mariolatry may have descended from the Minoan palace of Knossos.39.1

As regards the third group in my classification, external symbols and liturgical objects, we might suppose that these mainly belong to the minutiæ of archæological study. A philosopher may ignore them as trivial facts; but they have been the cause of too much bloodshed and strife to be ignored by the history of religions, and the feelings they excite are still powerful enough to divide the churches and the sects of Christendom. Besides, if one religion borrows its symbols and sacred objects from another, it probably borrows much more besides. The use of candles and incense in churches, the fashion of certain ecclesiastic vestments, can be shown to have descended to us from a pre-Christian world. And it was quite natural that the new faith should take over the religious property of paganism, whatever at least it could receive without violation of its own essential principles. It is only the anthropological study of these particulars, apparently insignificant in themselves, that enables us to understand certain modern controversies, as for instance concerning incense, and also to appreciate the extraordinary tenacity with which the successive generations cleave to the smaller things of cult. These latter are felt to be part of the spell which is exercised upon us by an immemorial tradition, a spell that is all the stronger because it works upon the "subconscious" self; and those who maintain them are rarely aware of the aboriginal reason which prompts them. And often the question about the symbols or the sacred objects of worship, as distinct from the ideas and personalities, becomes obviously of prime importance for the comparison and classification of religions. Thus the distinction between iconic or idolatrous and aniconic or non-idolatrous cults is of deep significance, for it may correspond to the distinction between a more and a less anthropomorphic conception of the divinity, or to a belief that the embodiment of him in material objects is right and seemly or wrong and unseemly. The more spiritual a religion becomes, the greater is its inclination to dispense with the idol and even to reprobate it; the worshipper of Jahvé was thus set in antagonism to the surrounding tribes, and in the Iranian region the Zarathustrian votary to the worshipper of the Daevas. The history of Christianity in regard to this matter is familiar to us all: in spite of the vehement protests of its apostles and earlier propagandists who inherited the spiritual Judaic view, we know that all the efforts of the iconoclastic emperors could not suppress the veneration of images in the later period. Even in the Teutonic north, Christianity came, in the days before the Reformation, to assume an iconic character which is not accounted for by the ancestral tradition of our pagan forefathers: who certainly carved images, in spite of what Tacitus tells us, but do not appear to have been markedly idolatrous. We infallibly detect here the abiding influence of Greco-Roman paganism, in which idolatry had taken so deep a root, satisfying as it did the artistic-religious cravings of the people. We have records of the transformation of the old statues into Christian images; in an epigram we find Heracles pathetically complaining that he is forced to become St Luke:42.1 a beautiful head of Aphrodite in Athens is rudely stamped with the cross, perhaps to convert her into the Virgin:42.2 at the present day there exists in South Italy an image of a Madonna del Granato, holding a pomegranate, which by a curious chain of evidence can be traced with some probability back to the Hera of Argos, carved by Polycleitos.

Now the image may be regarded in two aspects: as a symbol merely bringing close to the sense the spiritual idea of divinity, and serving to stimulate the prayerful thought of the worshipper: or it may be venerated as the indwelling abode of the divinity, in which he habitually resides, or into which, by spells and blood-offerings, he may be compelled to enter. The first is the more spiritual and advanced point of view, the orthodox aspect of the image in the iconic churches of Christendom at most periods; and this is put forward as an apology for what may seem idolatry: we may note in passing that the same apology was put forward by the advanced champions of paganism. The second is the more primitive view, accepted at most periods by the people, and sometimes tolerated or even encouraged by certain of the churches: the idol is regarded as miraculous, as infused with divine power, perhaps itself the very divinity; and the uncultured Greeks who whipped the idol of Pan with squills if food was scarce,43.1 or bound the image of Aphrodite with cords to prevent it running away,43.2 the Breton smith mentioned by Renan, who threatened the saint's image with red-hot pincers to compel him to heal his son, the modern savage who smears his idols with blood,44.1 are to be classed together in the morphology of religion.

Idolatry in this sense is a higher form of fetichism, which, strictly defined, is the veneration of material objects, often shaped by art and handled in such a way as to endow them with divine potency, which bring good fortune to the owner. It is supposed to connote savagery, but survivals of it are found in most civilised communities, and we probably all inherit some faint impress of the fetichistic spirit, nor need we be startled if we find it in the higher religions.

In ancient Greece the fetich was common enough: sacred axes, sacred sceptres, pyramidical or cone-shaped stones, rudely hewn tree-stumps, are examples which we find in the literature and art of the historic or prehistoric periods; the most common kind of private fetich was the gem, carried as an amulet. This superstitious view of gems belonging to primitive faith has continued through many ages. Moreover, both in the public and private religion of Christendom in many periods, and even at the present time, we can easily recognise the fetichistic value of the sacred objects, relics, crucifixes; and the Bible itself might sometimes be carried as an amulet about the person to secure one from danger, and its modern use in the English legal oath, the witness "kissing the book," conforms to a fetichistic type of oath which was common in the primitive Teutonic communities.45.1 When Tertullian exclaims, "How great is the difference between the wood of the cross and the shapeless wooden emblems of Pallas or Ceres,"45.2 he is thinking generally of the wide difference between Christianity and Hellenic polytheism. As regards the attitude of the Christian and pagan worshippers towards these emblems of their cult which Tertullian mentions, we are not sure that any such general distinction could be drawn. The "adoration of the true wood of the cross," of which we have heard in recent times, if we merely consider the nature of the religious object and the value of the material thing for faith, must be called fetichistic: at least I know of no other word equally appropriate in the terminology of the science of religions. Doubtless the modern mind, in the performance of such ritual practices, can distinguish between the inanimate or material thing and the divine spirit which sanctifies it. But so also can the intelligent savage, who cares nothing for his piece of wood when he thinks the power-giving spirit has departed from it. The fetichism then of the higher religions and of the savage faith is morphologically the same; the vital difference lies in the conception of the divinity that is supposed to animate or sanctify the material thing.

It would be wrong to attribute the fetichistic proclivities discovered in the Christian communities wholly to the Hellenic or Mediterranean strain in our religion; for we must reckon with the survival among the later ritual-observances of the superstitions of the Northern peoples, and fetichism was certainly characteristic of the early Teutonic, Celtic, and Slavonic races. In this matter, as in others, we have to note that the puritanism of the early Church could not prevail against the strength of habit and immemorial tradition.

The illustration of this group of affinities may conclude with the observation that the most cherished emblem of our creed, the type of the cross itself, had already been in vogue as a religious symbol of certain of the earlier pagan peoples; it played a part in the ancient Egyptian47.1 and Assyrian ritual, and recently Dr Evans has revealed to us in the Palace of Minos in Crete a chapel of the cross dedicated to the worship of the divine mother.48.1 We can go no further than the surmise that the propagation of Christianity may have been assisted by the fact that the emblem of the new faith would not appear wholly unfamiliar to some of the converted races.

As regards the affinities discernible in respect of hieratic institutions, the organisation of churches, the relations of Church and State, I have only space to cite a few salient illustrations. The earliest Christian Church, a private religious society united by the bond of faith, the members contributing to each other's wants, with a simple democratic organisation of ecclesia and sacred officials, would not strike the contemporary Greco-Roman world as an unfamiliar phenomenon; for its family likeness to the Hellenic "thiasoi" or brotherhoods of cult was sufficiently obvious, and has often been commented on. They, like it, were often proselytisers, and, ignoring the barriers of caste, gens, and city, accepted in principle the religious fellowship of man. "It is well to consider all men friends and brothers, as being the family of God," says Apollonius,49.1 echoing the doctrine of the Stoics. The soil was ready prepared for the new cosmopolitan religion.

In considering the history of the hierarchy in Christendom, we are often obliged to turn our eyes back upon the pre-Christian period. For instance, the insistence on the apostolic succession in the various churches, a primary article of faith with many at the present time, is entirely in keeping with a very old Mediterranean tradition: for we find it not infrequently maintained in Hellenic paganism that the priest should descend directly from the god whom he serves, or from the first apostle who instituted the particular cult or mystery;50.1 we hear of the priest being qualified "by descent and by divine appointment."50.2 But in the earlier religious period the succession or descent was regarded in the linear and physical sense: this has become refined into the idea of a spiritual succession, maintained however by a continuity of physical though mystic contact. Here, as so often in the comparative study of religion, we have to note the physical and material ideas of the more primitive period maintaining themselves in the later but translated into a spiritual significance.

The relation between the priesthood and the State has been one of the burning questions of the secular and religious history of Europe. To understand fully all the features in the State organisation of the Church and the many points of controversy, we need often to go far back into the records of early Aryan and Mediterranean society. We may mark here and there in the pagan Anatolian region the emergence of the idea that the priest should be temporal lord,51.1 while in most early Aryan societies the subordination of the spiritual to the secular power appears to have been maintained. A study of the sagas of the North suggests the reflection that the struggle fought out to a definite decision at the Reformation had already been decided in the Teutonic North in the far-off days before Christianity;52.1 also that the secular character of the married English priesthood in our pre-Conquest period is only the reflex of old Teutonic custom.

The celibacy of the priesthood is, again, a question that has agitated and divided the churches, nor does it appear that we ourselves have finished with it. To trace its origin and inner significance, a wide anthropological study is necessary, and I may be able to return to it in another association in a later lecture. Within the history of the Church, we may trace back the religious ideas underlying the dogma of celibacy to the ascetic enthusiasm of the third and fourth centuries, and we may be right in connecting it with the growth of Mariolatry. But the original source of the phenomenon lies far in the background of our religion; the impulse to religious celibacy had long been congenial to the temperament of some of the Anatolian races. We find it powerful in the Judaic sect of the Essenians; and in the anthropology of primitive societies we are often confronted with the idea that the virgin body is the only fit organ for the full divine afflatus.

In another question of administration, in the position of women in regard to the ministry, we can trace the opposing forces of differing pre-Christian traditions.53.1 Their present total exclusion from sacred functions in all but a few sects shows the triumph of the Judaic rule sanctioned and insisted upon by St Paul; it is not at all in accordance with Teutonic or Greco-Roman religious custom; and in fact we find in the early centuries of the Church, when Greek influence was strongest, that certain offices of the ministry could be fulfilled by women; we even hear of a heretic sect in the fifth century that signalised itself by the orgiastic processions of the "priestesses of the Virgin Mary."54.1 It is still possible that the old Teutonic view in this matter may reassert itself.

If we try to give a complete account of any of the important institutions of the churches, infant baptism or the Roman confession for instance, we ought at least, before we can pronounce that any particular one is a spontaneous or a unique growth, to survey the religions contiguous to or immediately preceding Christianity. As regards the practice of confession, a usage which, as I hope to show, may be explained as connected with a ritual of purification, its institution cannot at least be regarded as a unique phenomenon in the early Church. A very simple form of it appears to have been known to the Judaic system, and it appears as a formal element in the Babylonian liturgy:54.2 as a spiritual relief to which a man might voluntarily resort, it was encouraged by the Delphic oracle;55.1 as part of the cathartic ritual which was preliminary to initiation it was required by the ordinances of the Samothracian Mysteries; and it is in an anecdote concerning these that we meet with the first example of the free Protestant spirit reprobating the practice.55.2 We may infer that it was uncongenial to the character and alien to the tradition of our Teutonic forefathers, in the record of whose pagan institutions there is no hint of it, and Alcuin complains of his Goths "that no one of the laity was willing to confess to the priests."55.3 It may well have been a spontaneous growth of southern Christianity; but it appears to have arisen first within the early monastic orders,55.4 and as these in their origin had certain affinities with the non-Christian mystic brotherhoods, where the practice was not unknown, it is possible that in this matter also a pre-Christian tradition was still of some effect. Or, if this is unlikely, we must maintain that like conditions evolve similar products over the whole area with which comparative religion deals; and the most striking resemblance to a Christian confessional is to be observed in the old Mexican ritual, if we can trust Sahagun.56.1 As regards the other suggested example, we should probably find, if we followed out the history and origin of infant baptism, that the pre-Christian tradition was a strong efficient force in the settlement of the question; there were urgent reasons at least why the rite should soon have come to be maintained by the early Church, for analogous rites whereby the new-born child was consecrated to the divinity were probably part of the hereditary tradition of most of the converted races. We know that many of the Hellenes had been in the habit of passing the infant solemnly round the fire, a purificatory and also consecrating process;57.1 the northern Teutons sprinkled the infant with water:57.2 and when Aristotle tells us that many of the barbarian tribes were in the habit of plunging the new-born into river-water, to harden the little ones, he is mistaking a religious for a secular practice.57.3 Looking at the baptism of the adult neophyte, we find interesting resemblances to the ceremonies of the pre-Christian mystic initiations; the idea commonly expressed in these latter, that the catechumen died to his old life and was born again, was eagerly adopted and developed by the later religion, and here as there left its imprint on the ritual: death and rebirth were actually simulated in the mystic service.57.4

The affinities between Christian and pagan ritual, in many cases no doubt the result of direct inheritance, demand a more detailed investigation than they have yet received, especially in respect of the festival calendar: even the early writers of the Church were of opinion that the feast of the Purification of the Virgin Mary in February, was a development of the old Roman Februalia instituted by Numa;58.1 and such names of Christian saints and bishops as Hilarion, Hilarius, attest the popularity of the Hilaria, the festival of Adonis in the last days of paganism. Much might be still discovered by a minute knowledge of the Greco-Roman records, combined with travel in Mediterranean lands and with personal observation of the ritual of feast- and fast-days in the remoter villages.58.2

Finally, there remains the question, of greater moment and perplexity than all the preceding, concerning the affinities of the Christian and pre-Christian religions in primary ideas and essential belief. To point out resemblances is not necessarily to ignore contrasts; only it is of more avail for present science to emphasise the former, as the latter are obvious enough and have always been emphasised. But we must guard against accepting too rashly the fact of resemblance for proof of actual origin; nor must we ignore the truth that two religions may be vitally different in effect, while they use the same materials of thought and belief. The subject demands great knowledge and critical insight, and I can only indicate here clues that have already been followed and might be followed further. There is probably no need to call to your notice the fact that the incarnation of the Godhead in human form was a familiar conception to the civilised and half-civilised races of the old world, and was attached equally to mythic personages as well as to actual men. That such a personality could serve as a mediator between man and the Supreme God was conceivable to the Hellenic, Egyptian, even the Latin imagination; and though the idea does not seem to have been woven into any fabric of faith by these races, it appears as a natural product in the higher stages of polytheism, and in many primitive and advanced societies it has dominated men's views concerning the person and position of the King.

More important still for the purposes of the religious comparison is the wide prevalence in the Mediterranean communities of the belief in the death and resurrection of the divinity: and this has been the theme of much recent anthropological investigation.60.1 This is not the time to examine into its origin and significance or to track out the various phenomena that illustrate and group themselves around it in the Mediterranean cults. I would merely call attention in passing to the fact that the belief existed, and was probably expressed in the pre-Christian ritual of St Paul's own city of Tarsos,61.1 and that it was especially strong in the Attis Mysteries of the Great Mother of Phrygia and Crete; we know that these were celebrated at a season which corresponded to the end of our Lenten period and the beginning of Easter, that they were preceded by fasting and began with lamentations, the votaries gathering in sorrow around the bier of the dead divinity; then followed the resurrection, and the risen god gave hope of salvation to the mystic brotherhood, and the whole service closed with the feast of rejoicing, the Hilaria.62.1 The Christian fathers themselves were struck with the deep resemblance between this and their own mystery, and they were tempted to attribute it to the diabolic spirit of parody. We may take the words of Firmicus Maternus,62.2 with which he concludes his description of such an Attis Mystery as I have outlined—"truly the devil has Christians of his own"—as the text of a very important chapter in comparative religion. We hear of a Christian convert in Crete being seduced by the fascinations of the Hilaria; and Phrygia, its ancestral home, was one of the earliest strongholds of Christianity. Here at least we may assume that the ancient dogma and ritual of the people was one of the predisposing causes operating in favour of the new.

The comparative student must also give careful consideration to what are called the eschatologic doctrines, the beliefs concerning posthumous happiness, salvation, and damnation, not only of the Judaic, but also of the Hellenic, Anatolian, and Egyptian religions: and especially to those of the Hellenic, for it was they that were most widely known in the area of the Greco-Roman world, and modern theory has at times endeavoured to trace back the apocalyptic literature of Christianity to Hellenic sources.63.1 The investigation would demand a careful study of the Eleusinian and the Orphic Mysteries, in both of which we find the pregnant idea that salvation after death depended on a religious act of faith or on a mystic communion with a divinity that might be attained on earth by a sacrament or other liturgical means: and the inquiry will include the question how far in these earlier systems the doctrine of salvation by faith was actually blended with any admixture of the ethical doctrine of salvation by works. And the problem, like many others in the scientific study of religion, will be found to concern philosophic as well as religious history.

The ideas attaching to sacrifice in the Mediterranean world have long been recognised as a vital subject of inquiry for the comparative science; and both the lower and the higher anthropology can contribute much that is essential to the full understanding of the evolution of the Christian doctrine concerning the divine sacrifice and the Holy Communion. I need not here enlarge on this subject, even by way of mere illustration, for I have already dealt with it, however inadequately, in a former paper:65.1 it is an intricate and fascinating theme and invites further research.

But for proving the revival on the new Christian soil of the older pre-Christian religious thought and aspiration, there is no special subject so fruitful as the study of Mariolatry. I have already suggested by way of illustration the possibility of such pagan titles as "Kore-Parthenos," the "Gods' mother," having exercised an abiding influence in exciting and shaping the nascent thought of earlier Christendom; and I affirmed that their prevalence corresponded to a prevailing religious bias which turned the minds of many of the peoples in the old world to cleave affectionately to the mother-goddess or to the divine maid. Apart from mere titles, the student of the latter days of paganism is forced to note at almost every point the deep impress of such ideas and the enthusiasm they evoked. In all the leading Greek mysteries, the Mother and the Maid held a dominant position, and the Orphic brotherhoods had ranged the Mother by the side of the Son-God and the Father-God; and even in the state-cults of the ancient centres of Hellenic civilisation, the maternal character of the divine power had long been cherished. Finally, the Phrygian religion of the Mother, to which even Mithraism, a pre-eminently masculine or paternal religion, was obliged to accommodate itself, had captured the greater part of the Greco-Roman world; and was certainly very influential in the districts of Asia Minor visited by St Paul and in every one of the cities of the Seven Churches. The sentiment it evoked is expressed by the words of a poet of the Middle Attic comedy: "For those who have true knowledge of things divine, there is nothing greater than the Mother; hence the first man who became civilised founded the shrine of the Mother."66.1 This then is a leading factor in the religious psychology of the converted nations with which we must reckon.

We cannot, in accordance with the laws of human nature, suppose that a religious tradition of such hereditary power as this could wholly lose its force under a changed creed. The gaps in the record will probably make it impossible to supply a detailed and geographical statement showing how in the various communities of the ancient cult the personality of the pre-Christian goddess was fused gradually with the ideal image of the Virgin-Mother of Christ. Only a few suggestive facts in the development and organisation of Mariolatry may be mentioned here. The heretic Montanists of Phrygia were charged with deifying the Virgin and believing that one of their leaders was united in a mystic marriage with her, a belief natural to Phrygian paganism; and their founder Montanus is said to have originally been a priest of Cybele.67.1 The mother of Constantine, the Empress Helena, who is supposed to have been of Bithynian origin, was praised for decking the grotto of Bethlehem with sacred gifts as the shrine of the Virgin;68.1 it is noteworthy that her earliest recorded chapel should be a grotto or cave; for it was in such underground shrines that the Phrygian Mother was commonly worshipped in her own land. Another striking analogy to the ancient ritual of the mother-goddess is presented by the feast called the κοίμησις and ἀνάληψις τῆς Θεοτόκου, first mentioned by Andreas of Crete (*circ.* 650 A.D.), but probably in existence long before his time: the Mother of God dies and rises again in the Assumption. It would be of special interest if we could discover that this ritual first became canonical in Crete, the home of Andreas; for in Crete as in Cyprus, where the Virgin succeeded to the name of Aphrodite, we have traces of a similar rite in which the goddess Aphrodite was laid out as dead on a bier and was afterwards raised to life.69.1

And is it nothing more than a coincidence that in the same city of Ephesus, where during St Paul's visit the fanatics raised a tumult in behalf of their Virgin Artemis, some six centuries later the people with equal ecstasy hailed the decision of the Synod that proclaimed the Virgin-Mother of God (Θεοτόκος)? The mention of Ephesus suggests another consideration of the greatest importance for the study of the development and propagation of the Christian dogma concerning the virginity of the Mother of God. The Virgin-birth, an idea which has long been a stumbling-block to science, and which has recently been pronounced by some to be unessential to Christianity, was a dogma that could easily be understood and even eagerly accepted by the converts of Anatolia69.2 and the Greek world. In Ephesus itself the ancient goddess had been imagined in some sense as a maternal or generative divinity, yet also as a virgin, in whose ritual, conducted partly by a priesthood of monks, a strong rule of austerity and chastity was enforced.70.1 The great Phrygian Mother was herself, according to a native legend, miraculously conceived, and there are grounds for suggesting that she was occasionally regarded as a virgin.70.2 The evidence indeed concerning such ideas in the pre-Christian cults is always confused, casual, and often contradictory, with no power apparently in themselves to develop a fixed dogma of faith. It would be in fact unreasonable to maintain that the Christian doctrines concerning the Virgin-Mother could have been evoked merely by the spontaneous demand of the Anatolian or Greek converts. But we may affirm that when that doctrine was presented to them, their own traditions had prepared their imaginations to receive it as congenial. We meet in the late pagan literature passages in praise of virginity as a divine quality quite as ecstatic and extravagant as many in the Christian fathers.71.1 Many of the nations had long cherished the ideal of a virgin goddess; most had been devotees of the Divine Mother. The successful propagation of Christianity may have owed much to the means which it possessed for satisfying these two sentiments and for reconciling them in a primary article of faith. Then, we must certainly ascribe the exaltation of Mary in the Church of the first six centuries to the enthusiasm engendered by the older goddess-worships. Alexandria may have contributed much more than we have already noted; and more than one writer has explored the deep indebtedness of the developed Mariolatry to the older figure of Isis.72.1 The extravagance of an enthusiasm that was rooted in old pagan sentiment occasionally engendered heresies. Besides the records concerning the Montanist, of which the significance has already been noticed, most interesting and valuable for our purpose is the sermon of Epiphanius against the heresy of the Collideriani,72.2 wild women who devoted themselves to the worship of Mary, and whose orgiastic service he describes and reprobates: in their processions they appear to have drawn the Virgin round in a car strewn with raiment, and they solemnised a sacrament with bread: and he adds that they came from Thrace, the immemorial home of fanatic women and of the goddess "Artemis the Queen," to whom also offerings of corn were made.72.3 The procession of a goddess in a car was probably part of an old Thrako-Phrygian ceremonial, and we hear of a sacramental eating of bread in the service of Cybele.

We may finally note that the enthusiastic literature devoted to the pre-Christian Divine Mother and Maid and to the Virgin-Mother of God is the same in quality and tone. The prayer addressed to Isis in the story of Apuleius reminds us of a Christian hymn of praise; and the older liturgical or literary expressions would naturally colour the later.73.1

Another question with which the comparative study of Christianity is concerned touches the evolution of the Trinitarian idea.73.2 Here again it is necessary carefully to sift the phenomena of the contiguous religions, to consider whether they present such a conception at all, and whether in any of them it had gained sufficient vividness and power to be likely to evoke a dogma of religious metaphysic. Moreover, to understand the complete genesis of the Christian doctrine, we must trace out the idea of divine emanations in the Mediterranean and the East; for the religions of the Iranian and even the Greek world present us with parallels to the process whereby the Holy Spirit becomes in relation to the personal God a distinct though closely attached personality. In the Zoroastrian ritual the Fravashi or Soul of Ahura receives reverence,74.1 and in Greek speculation and even cult the Θεοῦ Πρόνοια or Divine Providence is sometimes regarded as an individual and personal power;75.1 nor is the conception of a plurality of beings within the limits of the same personality unfamiliar to primitive thought. The subject is one of the most intricate in the field of religious study, and the more hopeful investigation of it would demand anthropological study in its widest sense, combined with a knowledge of the later Greek metaphysic which has clearly left its impress on our doctrine.

I will close these illustrations with the most obvious example of the contribution of anthropological study to our knowledge of actual Christendom. One of the most fruitful offshoots of the older Hellenic system was hero-worship, which itself may have arisen as a development of ancestor-cult. At first confined to the mythic figures of the past, it came to be applied to founders of colonies, legislators, and even to athletes; in its final development in the last centuries before Christ it was chiefly consecrated to kings and dynasts, the founders of religious societies, men of science, and political benefactors. The divine worship of the mortal, an idea abhorrent to Judaism, and not accepted by the severer Zoroastrian, was part of the state system of earlier and later Egypt, and was finally imposed on the Greco-Roman world. The soil in which it had most rankly flourished was Greek, and Greece and Anatolia were crowded with chapels consecrated to recently living men or to faded figures who were supposed to have once lived on earth, some of them perhaps actual ancestors, some imaginary personages of the epic or legendary world, some merely functional divinities of subordinate departments, like the hero of the ploughshare or the tutelary hero of the potters. This growth of polytheism had struck its roots so deeply that Christianity, in spite of its monotheistic ideal, was unable to eradicate it. The ancient hero may sometimes be lurking under the later disguise of the saint: the mediæval guild, like the Attic fraternity of potters, had its sacred tutelary patron; and it is curious to observe that in the matter of canonisation the Pope came to play exactly the same part as the Delphic oracle had played in the public consecration of the hero-cult: the divine authorisation is given or withheld by the vicar or agent of God. The importance of this inherited tradition in determining our religious estimate of historical Christendom is of the highest: for whatever may have been or may be the orthodox dogma of the Church concerning the status of the saint, such worship inevitably means polytheism from the point of view of the popular faith: and we gather that in many outlying communities of Christendom, as of the ancient Greek world, the lower cult overshadows the higher. And this is one of the most salient and sure examples that we can quote of the direct influence of the older religions upon the later. This special influence is mainly Greek, though the pagan North, the Celtic and Lithuanian, and perhaps the Teutonic peoples, have contributed much to the tradition of saint-worship.

The illustrations given may suffice as a sketch of the various applications of a comparative method to the problems that the phenomena of Christianity offer to the student. In the choice of illustration I may seem to have ignored the strength of the Judaic element in determining the evolution; but I have considered it unnecessary to touch on this, as it has long been the familiar theme of scientific theology. I have also ventured to suggest that our own religious history should be traced back to the period of our ancestral paganism. And I would strongly recommend to the student of comparative religion in England a devoted attention to the world of the Norse Saga: for this has been strangely and fatally neglected by our English system of culture, with grievous loss to our poetic imagination, and to our knowledge of the early law and the religious institutions and temperament of our ancestors. Such a work as Golther's *Handbuch der germanischen Mythologie* shows us what a harvest may be reaped in that field for the science of religion. The subject in its own right claims our interest, and certain phenomena in the old Teutonic religion, its fatalistic ideas, its eschatologic beliefs concerning a "day of judgment," demand consideration in the light of more advanced creeds. On the other hand it may be wrong to attribute to it any direct influence on the inner development of Northern Christianity; for there may be reason for the view that, when the new religion conquered the Teutonic North, it found there in some sense a religious vacuum, the old ritual and faith having lost its vitality and hold; and certainly our ancestral paganism made no such struggle to survive as did the Greco-Roman. Nevertheless the history of its institutions may be necessary, as has been suggested already, to explain the struggle between Church and State in Teutonic lands; and, further, it is only the pages of the Norse Saga-book that can yield us an answer to the question whether we may not have inherited from remote times a certain average racial law of religious temperament resulting in a characteristic attitude towards matters of religion that may have determined our religious history. If the answer were affirmative and definite, the fact would have a practical no less than a speculative importance. At least we shall not know ourselves completely in this or in other matters if we continue to think that Greece and Rome and Palestine are our sole intellectual and spiritual ancestors; in fact we may say that no account of the history of Christianity in any European State can be real and complete unless we can get back to the pre-Christian past of that community.

Yet, while making full allowance for the influence of special ancestral traditions, those who work on the lines which have been indicated in the illustrations of method which I have selected, will acquire the ever-growing conviction that Hellas has dominated the creed as she has dominated the intellectual history of Christendom; that the new faith, in spite of its fierce or contemptuous intolerance of the past, was only able to transform but not to abolish the Mediterranean tradition: that in fact Sir Henry Maine's often quoted aphorism, while by no means wholly true, was truer in respect of religious history than he himself was aware.

I have been speaking hitherto mainly on the relations of anthropology to the comparative study of religion. And it may be well now to point out that anthropology, as I have tried to define and distinguish its functions, though an essential part, is only a part of the whole. For we must know not only the past but the present conditions, not only the embryology but the perfected growth. And, again, we compare religions not merely to test theories of origin, ancestry, and indebtedness, but also to form the proper estimate of each one, and to correct the one-sided judgment that is always quick to pronounce this phenomenon or feature in any particular system as unique. If the comparison reveals more divergences than parallels, the result is no less important. And the comparative method should be applied not merely to ritual, liturgy, hieratic institutions, legends, and dogmas, but also to the varying phenomena and expressions of the religious temperament in the various races. Only the study of the latter can enable us to test the living force of a faith, the degree with which it possesses the national mind; and such a study is only possible when a nation has produced a rich religious literature or monuments of art embodying the public and private worship and religious sentiment. We know what we have gained by the discovery of the sacred books of the East, by the interpretation of the Babylonian inscriptions, and from their revelation to us in the Vedic, Iranian, and Mesopotamian cult-centres of a fervour as deep and passionate as any that we find in Hebraic or Christian writings. On the other hand, when a religion has passed away, as is the case with that of pre-Hellenic Rome, without leaving any articulate expression of its inner life, our knowledge of it can be superficial only, confined to mere ritual, fragments of liturgies, and the externals of cult.

A dispassionate and uncontroversial study of that which is at least one of the greatest forces in human society cannot but be interesting, and fruitful also for other branches of inquiry, such as the history of early law and morals, of which in many primitive communities the religion is the only record. It may even solve certain problems concerning the early migrations of races, as I have been convinced by the investigation of various Greek cults. In England the trained workers in this field are still unfortunately few, perhaps because a certain latent prejudice, born of religious partisanship, is not yet extinct, and may act somewhat as a deterrent. I have avoided hitherto alluding to any of the practical and controversial considerations which the methodical pursuit and propagation of this science may excite, though I am well aware that its practical effects may be of high importance; but they are not immediately our concern at present. There is, however, one such consideration that it is pertinent to touch on before concluding the survey of the methods and functions of this branch of historical inquiry, which deals much with origins and with the evolution of higher forms of religion from the lower. Discoveries of origins may appear to affect the validity of a creed or certain articles of creed. That this is actually the case in regard to the great problem with which the illustrations I have put before you are mainly concerned, namely, the genesis of Christianity, has been recently frankly admitted by a leading dignitary of the Roman Church: who, moved by a rumour of anthropological research, has promptly turned it to the profit of his cause by maintaining that the Roman ritual and communion gains in force and validity by the discovery that it has inherited and absorbed the religious thought and practice of ancient Greece and Rome. On the other hand, others may find the exposition of the so-called pagan elements in the essence of Christianity repugnant to their sentiment; and hence are inclined to accept the dictum "that origin does not affect validity." I imagine the facts of religious psychology make somewhat against this aphorism. But it only concerns the science of comparative religion, because in the history of creeds validity has been very often found to maintain itself mainly by an appeal to origin; and as our science, to reiterate, is much concerned with origins, it is indirectly concerned with those claims of validity that support themselves by such an appeal.

Another cause of the paucity of workers in this field is the complexity and difficulty of the subject, which can be handled successfully only by the advanced and mature student. The pre-requisites of competence are an exact philological as well as an archæological training, with a view to the proper appreciation both of texts and monuments; secondly, a general acquaintance with the problems and history of philosophy, and especially of ethics, and with the history of early social institutions and law; thirdly, a comprehensive study of anthropology. To this must be added a sympathetic and minute knowledge of at least two of the great world-religions, whereby alone a critical insight into the essential and significant phenomena of the religious experiences of our race can be obtained. The comparative science of religion has now become possible, thanks partly to the labours of philological specialists in the ancient languages of Europe and Asia, and partly to the organisation of anthropological travel.

Let me conclude with remarking that subdivision of labour is imperative in this field: and it is especially in Oxford that the opportunities for the requisite preliminary training are plentiful. It would be a gain for more than science if we could see a group of mature students organised here exploring the various departments of this complex subject in co-operation and with mutual assistance.

LECTURE III
THE RITUAL OF PURIFICATION
AND THE CONCEPTION OF PURITY:
THEIR INFLUENCE ON RELIGION,
MORALITY, AND SOCIAL CUSTOM

Among all the varied religious acts of man, there is probably none that has been so widely prevalent throughout the different races of mankind as the ritual of purification, nor does any idea seem to have possessed so strong a legislative power in the various departments of our life as the concept of purity. We can trace it back to instincts that we appear to share with the higher animals, and we can track it upwards through the complex rites of the higher religions. The record presents us with a vast mass of phenomena which, as far as I am able to discover, have not yet been reduced to system or unified by any constructive theory of evolution. In this lecture I venture to attempt the systematisation of the subject, first giving a brief summary of the main facts which are well known to the students of primitive anthropology and comparative religion and which confront us in nearly all the societies that have been explored.

In the stage of our conscious life which we may call, relatively to man's growth, primeval, certain bodily acts and states and certain material substances are regarded as unclean and impure, likely to imprint a stain upon the person. It is impossible here to attempt to enumerate all the examples, and it is enough to mention a few that are salient and typical. The generative processes of life, the states and activities of the male and especially the female organism connected with them, the bodily changes incident on puberty, are among the most familiar phenomena with which the idea of impurity in some peculiar sense has been universally associated. A chief centre or "nidus" of impurity is child-birth; but still more dangerously impure is its counterpart, death and all the phenomena of death. In respect of child-birth the idea is fading away from our civilised consciousness; but it has left a deep deposit in our conscious or subconscious self in regard to death. The material substance that has been most generally felt to be impure is blood; the curious feeling that the mere mention of the word often excites in certain modern people is a faint reflex of the savage mental state in respect to the thing; and the influence of this disposition upon advanced society raises the most interesting question in which comparative law, ethics, and religion are jointly concerned, and which will be considered later. To continue our enumeration we may not find that the objects of the inanimate world outside ourselves are usually regarded by primitive thought as in themselves impure, but all or most of them are capable of catching the infection from ourselves, from death or child-birth for instance: hence it may be necessary to break or destroy or purify the utensils and furniture of the house where a death or a birth has occurred. At a somewhat more advanced stage, certain food-stuffs come to rank as impure, and a complicated code of "tapu" is established for specially sanctified persons. Then we are confronted, but not apparently in the most primitive period, with the distinction between pure and impure animals, which also dictates certain rules and practices of diet.

On the other hand certain natural things may come to be regarded as specially "pure," whether on the ground of a certain intrinsic quality, because for instance they are bright and lustrous, or from the fact that they were habitually used for cathartic or cleansing processes, as fire, water, odorous wood or spices, or substances which emitted a pungent odour such as sulphur. Such objects "are used in ritual," says Jamblichus,91.1 "because they are specially full of the divine nature." But the psychic phenomena and the corresponding acts with which we are dealing may be well suspected of descending from an age at which no definite concept of a divine nature had as yet arisen, an age not yet perhaps even animistic, for in their crudest form they do not seem necessarily to imply any articulate system of belief in a world of ghosts and spirits. And this reflection brings us to the first question of importance, what this primitive concept of purity and impurity really is, and what were the sensations from which it was evolved. Nothing is more difficult to describe than simple sensations, but it is possible to distinguish one from another. And we must distinguish between the modern feeling about cleanliness and the primitive feelings which we are considering. That "cleanliness is next to godliness" is an aphorism suggested no doubt by sensations fundamentally akin to these; but many a savage who is most particular about "impurity" cares little or nothing for what we call "cleanliness." We consider that the cleansing acts we ourselves perform are purely hygienic or pleasure-giving, partly connected with the instinct of self-preservation, and some of them we find performed by other animals than man.

But the savage ritual of purification does not by any means tend necessarily to self-preservation, but at times may lead to self-destruction, and no hygienic or utilitarian or secular considerations will carry us far in explaining the cathartic code of Leviticus or the Zend-Avesta, or Buddhism, or the impurity of tabooed animals. These codes, while some of their prescriptions may be such as modern utilitarian ideas might dictate, are obviously instinct with religious or superstitious beliefs, and to explain the distinction between the pure and the impure animals would need a long excursus into primitive religion; the distinction is certainly not one between wholesome and unwholesome, or pleasant and unpleasant, meat.

We may probably discover the nature of the instinct underlying much of the cathartic custom-law by taking as our typical example the savage feeling about blood. Evidence from almost every society in the world yields proof that the stain of blood is the primary impurity that needs a purifying ritual: hence arose a body of rules that were a burden upon domestic life, hence the elaborate purifications of warriors after battle or of the individual homicide. Such rules in no way remind us of the natural desire to take a bath at the end of a warm field-day: the savage purifications after battle may last for weeks; it is recorded that a North American Indian tribe was extirpated because it needed a month to wipe off the stain of a single conflict, while their enemies needed only a week for that purpose and therefore had the advantage of three weeks' start in preparing for the next attack. The sense-instinct that suggests all this is probably some primeval terror or aversion evoked by certain objects, as we see animals shrink with disgust at the sight or smell of blood. The nerves of savage man are strangely excited by certain stimuli of touch, smell, taste, sight: the specially exciting object is something that we should call "mysterious," "weird," or, still more expressively, "uncanny." To the primitive mind nothing was more uncanny than blood, and there are people still who faint at the sight of it: for "the blood is the life," life and death are the great primeval mysteries, and all the physical substances that are associated with the inner principle of either partake of this mysteriousness. For the savage, what is mysterious is also dangerous and not to be lightly handled or approached. Now, the man who incurs such stain not merely is exposed to some unaccountable danger himself, but he is able to infect others by contagion; he spreads a sort of miasma, he is the conducting vehicle of a dangerous spiritual electricity—mere metaphors, which, however, may enable us to catch something of the primitive thought. Such a man therefore must avoid communion with his fellows for a time, must be "tabooed"; and will naturally endeavour to remove the "tapu" or dangerous "miasma" by some magic rites of cleansing or release. The kinsmen of the recently dead in all primitive societies are impure, because they have come into contact with death, the chief source of all impurity; therefore they must be isolated, and, until they are purified, must wear some badge or external mark—which we call "mourning"—to warn others against approaching them. The "tapu" still remains in civilised communities; we abstain from intruding on the bereaved family, though we give a different motive for our keeping aloof. It so often happens that in such matters we act as the savage acts; but we must abandon for a time our normal way of looking at things in order to imagine his. To us a corpse may be an object of aversion, and it is in some degree contagious; but our view of it, when we are cool, is secular and scientific: while the primitive aspect of it is supranormal and mystic, and the contagion is something spiritual and incalculably dangerous. In the Zend-Avesta we find an interesting special application of this idea: the defiling power of the dead varies directly according to the sanctity or rank of the deceased; thus it is greatest in the corpse of the priest, somewhat less in that of a warrior, and least in that of the husbandman:97.1 *corruptio optimi pessima*: the most sacred person can defile the most, because he is charged with the most mysterious and therefore dangerous potency. The Latin term "sacer" has the double meaning of "holy" and "accursed": from the same Greek root, $\alpha\gamma$, spring a word connoting holiness and a word meaning "pollution." Primeval thought or feeling holds together in a vague unity ideas that afterwards differentiate themselves and even become antithetical. The same power of radiating dangerous influence, supposed to attach to the holy man, the polluted man and the polluting thing, brought them originally under the same dim conception.

It would not repay us here to endeavour to trace out and explain all the minutiæ of this superstition: the long lists of pure and impure things that one might compile do not disclose any single regulative idea, and nothing is more baffling than the eccentricities of prejudice and terror. But this superstition often proceeds with a logic of its own: as a corpse is most unclean, and all who touch it are impure, therefore dogs and wolves and carrion birds are impure and must not be eaten: and anything that however distantly reminds us of danger and death, such as quarrelsome acts and words, may come to be rigidly prohibited during a ritual of purification. As blood is primevally impure, therefore any substance analogous to it or of the same colour might be regarded as ill-omened, such as beans or pomegranates. The same kind of sensational aversion will cause malodorous substances to be regarded usually as unclean; therefore food of an evil savour, or such as leaves unpleasant traces in the person, will often be tabooed by certain strict sects.99.1 There is also a certain common-sense discoverable in the distinction between substances on the ground of their greater or less susceptibility to spiritual contagion: earthen pots, for instance, have been often considered more easily infected than metal, and need longer purification, liquid substances more dangerous conductors than dry. "Should the dry mingle with the dry," says Ahura Mazda in a conversation with Zarathustra, "how soon all this material earth of mine would be only one Peshôtanu," which is as much as to say that the earth would become a charnel-house of impurity. And Darmesteter99.2 remarks, in commenting on this verse, "Nowadays in Persia, the Jews are not allowed to go out of their house on a rainy day, lest the religious impurity conducted through the rain should pass from the Jew to the Mussalman." We have here a view of contagion that seems to agree with that of modern science, only the latter is physical, the former mystic or spiritual. Again, the choice of substances used for purification was not dictated by the modern idea of a cleansing quality, but by a certain superstitious logic which we can sometimes detect. If liquid substances have a natural affinity for contagion, then if we take them while they are uninfected and use them for lustration, they will easily absorb the impurities of our own persons and rid us of them; therefore the modern savage or the ancient Greek might think it desirable to daub himself with clay or mud to wash away his taint: and from this example we see how distinct these primeval lustral processes are from the modern hygienic washing, to which nevertheless they often bear a close resemblance. By a similar reasoning we may explain an inconsistency that occasionally appears in the cathartic ritual; a substance impure as food might be used for purposes of lustration: for instance, we find garlic used as a cathartic in the worship of the Phrygian god Mên at Athens.101.1 Fire, the universal purifier, may have been accredited with this power by right of its own nature, but partly in all probability because it was believed to dry up miasma and damp infection.101.2

In the Zend-Avesta code, after drying for a whole year under the light of the sun, the corpse at last becomes pure; for by the same natural instinct that caused the aversion to blood, the sun's light comes to be regarded as the purest thing in the world: meat cooked by its warmth is more sanctified than fire-cooked meat; and certain acts and states of man have a greater defilement in the sun's face.

So far I have been trying to present the phenomena without reference to any definite religious belief, to express them as far as possible in terms of simple sensation; for, as was said at the beginning of the discussion, it is possible that they have descended from a pre-religious age. We may now ask how the baneful influence of the impure thing in this primeval stage of thought was supposed to work, unassisted by any spiritual agency such as spirit or god. We may suppose that it produced its results indirectly by depressing the vital energies of the man who was the victim of the superstition: the savage might believe that it worked directly, by some mysterious law of luck, paralysing a man's force and spoiling his hunting and fighting. This idea of a spontaneous mesmeric power of evil that certain things possess seems to glimmer through the verse in the Zend-Avesta. "Here am I," says an unlucky man to those whom he meets, "one who has touched the corpse of a man and who is powerless in mind, powerless in tongue, powerless in hand; do make me clean."103.1 Is it an illusion to believe that we have here penetrated to the psychological root of the whole matter? And here there is no direct reference to spirit or god.

But at an early period such reference was made, and it was then that this cathartic ritual really started on a momentous career. When the doctrine of animism became firmly established, it attracted the ritual and the ideas associated with it, and the animistic imprint upon them can still be traced even in the higher religions. A dangerous spirit was supposed to abide in the impure thing and to be evoked by the unclean act; the potency which in the primeval stage of feeling had been perhaps regarded merely as something mysteriously baneful and "uncanny," now becomes personal and intelligible and can be dealt with and exorcised by certain efficacious rules. The stain of blood on the homicide attracts the ghost of the slain to pursue him, certain foods are impure because evil spirits attach to them, disease is specially their work, and a veritable pandemonium gathers around the corpse, the woman in child-birth, and the new-born child. Illustrations showing how this demoniac faith has pervaded the thought of the world are broadcast in the records of primitive man as well as in the higher literature of our race, the Vedic and Iranian sacred books, the New Testament, the Pythagorean, Platonic, and Neoplatonic texts. In the view of the Zend-Avesta, which regards the whole universe as an overcharged battery of spiritual electricity, a single careless act of accidental uncleanliness is a cosmic catastrophe: legions of "drugs" or devils start up at once into existence to destroy the world of righteousness.104.1 Plato, though on the whole he preserves his sanity in the matter, is under the dominion of similar ideas, and Neoplatonism reverts back to the savage view, believing that the chief aim of ἀγνείαι, or purifications, was to drive the evil spirits out of certain kinds of food.105.1

The deep animistic colouring that the conception we are analysing came at a very early time to acquire may be responsible for a very important event in the history of religion: the evolution, namely, of the dualistic principle, the idea of the antagonism between good and evil spirits, the germ of which we can already detect in the animistic stage which may have preceded the faith in high personal gods. If the impure things and acts are impregnated with evil spirits, it is natural to suppose that the pure are the abode of the good, and these are contrary the one to the other. It may have required a very long period for a clear belief in the good spirit to crystallise; for to the very primitive mind all spirits are mysteriously dangerous, even the ghosts of one's dearest kinsmen. Still, the ancestral spirits make on the whole for righteousness, and can be given the position of guardians of the purification code. Thus the New Caledonians avert the wrath of the ghosts of their ancestors by washing, fasting, and chastity:106.1 the ancient Greek might pray or sacrifice to a vague animistic company of θεοὶ Ἀποτρόπαιοι or Μειλίχιοι, regarded perhaps as ghosts of the lower world, to avert the impure omen or to wash off the taint of blood.

Finally, the conception of purity comes under the dominion of the higher faith in a personal god. In Greece, Apollo and Zeus attach to themselves the ritual and the associated ideas; in Persia the whole complex code of purity is established by Ahura Mazda; in Israel by Jahvé, who enforces the minutest details of the law with insistence on the purity of God.106.2 In Babylonian as in Vedic religion, the fire-god is pre-eminently the purifier, a name which is attached particularly to Agni, and we find in the Babylonian liturgical texts the prayer,107.1 "May the torch of the shining fire-god cleanse me." Nor does Buddhism appear to differ from Leviticus or the Zend-Avesta in respect of the complications of its cathartic rules and the importance it attached to them. The Buddhist missionary, I-Tsing, exhorts the faithful to observe the elaborate prescriptions of the Buddha, "because," as he naively puts it, "gods and spirits get disgusted with our ways of wearing garments and eating food." With this abundance of testimony before us, we are all the more surprised to find that very little is forthcoming from the records of our own ancestral paganism. We can scarcely believe that our Teutonic ancestors were destitute of the idea of lustration, and that their cleanliness and chastity, attested by the Roman writers and still more clearly by their own sagas, were virtues of purely secular origin. And in fact we have certain records of Teutonic ritual that seem to point to cathartic ideas: "After the goddess Nerthus had gone on her annual procession round the villages," as Tacitus informs us,108.1 "her chariot and garments and her own person were solemnly washed in the waters of a sacred lake, as if the holy divinity had been polluted by her intercourse with men." It is also possible that the custom still prevalent in the Teutonic populations of Europe, of leaping over the bonfire on midsummer's eve, is the relic of a ceremony of fire-lustration performed before the beginning of harvest.108.2 Doubtless also they had the same rules as those prevailing in nearly all communities, whether civilised or uncivilised, concerning the purity of temples; for we have record of an Icelandic law that the "Holy Place of Peace" was not to be defiled by blood or any human uncleanness.108.3 Still, though other evidence pointing in the same direction might be gathered, it seems clear that the burden of the cathartic ritual did not weigh heavily on the consciences of our fathers when the dawn of their history begins. I am not aware of any indication, for instance, that they regarded formal lustration after bloodshed to be obligatory or desirable. And their comparative freedom in regard to such ceremonies is a fact of great importance with which we must reckon in our estimate of our later spiritual history. We may at the same time believe, on general grounds, that they also had at some remoter epoch passed through a period of bondage to the same ideas and the same formalities that we find so generally prevalent in other kindred and alien races.

The more interesting side of the inquiry now presents itself, the question about the influence that these cathartic ideas may have exercised upon religion, morality, and law. We may endeavour, for the sake of systematisation, to maintain this tripartite classification, although we find it becoming more and more illusory the further our investigation travels back to the earlier social life of man.

But before attempting to survey the special facts that present themselves within these three departments, it is well to note one phenomenon that concerns religion and morality in equal measure, and is of perhaps greater importance than all others in the varied process of the evolution of the cathartic idea. We have mainly been dealing so far with facts that seem to belong to the most primitive deposit of human consciousness and not properly to be ethical in the modern sense at all: the stain of blood, even incurred by ruthless murder, the stain of childbirth and the sexual processes, the contagion of the corpse, are all for the same reason "suspect" to primitive man because they involve vague and mysterious danger, not because they are associated with the concept of sin. Nor does this latter concept necessarily enter in, even when a more articulate animism has taken possession of the superstition, and the impurity means the presence of an evil spirit: the leper, the man who has come into contact with the dead, the blood-stained murderer, are all regarded as suffering from the same trouble, though in greater or lesser degree. The idea of purity and impurity, in fact, whether corporeal and external or whether spiritual in the sense of its association with the world of spirits, is still non-ethical, and we must not apply our moral standards to it until a later stage. It arrives at this stage and at its higher significance for morality when it has evolved the conception of a pure heart, a pure soul. And that this latter, which is one of the most pregnant of the concepts of developed ethics, was actually evolved from the primitive ritualistic and demoniac superstition can, I believe, be proved by the evidence, and accords with a well-known psychologic law of early thought.

We deceive ourselves if we are content to say that terms such as "pure heart," "pure soul" are mere metaphors. The theory of metaphors is a refuge for those who do not understand, or who do not wish to understand, religious history, and much might be said of the far-reaching effects of this fallacy of interpretation. The soul was not called "ψυχή" or "animus" or "spiritus" by mere metaphor: nor was the phrase "white liver" a metaphor for the people who first applied it to the coward. Primitive man may be the victim of false analogy and association of ideas, but these mental processes mean for him something other than metaphor means for us. It is not by way of metaphor that the modern Basuto speaks of his heart "being black and dirty," that is, "impure" or "sad," the same word being used for corporeal impurity, sadness, and sin.112.1 The colour of the impure act or bodily state is, so to speak, transferred inwards: if the act involves a physical stain, then, as things, words, and thoughts are so closely correlated in early psychology, the term "unclean word," "unclean thought" expresses a literal belief: gradually, as the concept of mind and soul becomes more and more immaterial, we may reach the spiritual concept of mental purity which is of value for modern ethics. The example quoted above reveals the Basuto at the half-way point in this evolution: and a certain North-American Indian tribe, whose customs have been recorded by Miss Alice Fletcher, appears to have reached the same mental stage; in her paper called the "Shadow of a Ghost Lodge," she mentions that the kinsmen who sit together isolated from others and mourning the dead for a period must rigidly abstain from any tales of fighting or "bad words," they must forget old injuries and cancel all grudges. The mental process that leads to this excellent *tapu* may be stated thus: the mourners are in a condition of deep impurity which they are endeavouring to cleanse away; quarrelling, vindictive speech, and memories would intensify the impurity, because all these are associated with bloodshed and death. This analogy may serve to explain the curious rule prevailing at Athens that anyone who laid a suppliant-bough on the altar in the Eleusinion during the period of the Eleusinian Mysteries was liable to the penalty of death or a heavy fine.114.1 I would suggest that the underlying thought is the same: the laying the suppliant-bough indicated a grievance and was a legally quarrelsome act, and therefore a violation of the purity of the solemn season. It was probably a similar chain of reasoning that induced the Greeks and other races of the higher religion to enforce silence before and during the sacrifice, not merely in order that the priest should not be disturbed by the chatter of the crowd; for the word used for this sacred silence is εὐφημία, "auspicious speech": it is obvious that the original motive of the rule was to guard against the utterance of any impure word that might produce an ill-omened condition of mind in the congregation.

Of this development of the idea of spiritual from that of ritualistic purity, the language of certain of the higher races affords the same indication as we find in the Basuto phrase: the Latin "purus" and the Greek καθαρός and φοῖβος themselves have an original material or physical significance; the blood that is shed and the unburied corpse emit a "miasma," a defiling atmosphere charged with dangerous spirits, and the same word μίασμα comes to denote a spiritual corruption of the soul: touching a corpse is called "sin" in the Zend-Avesta;115.1 and it is significant that the same word which is used to express the material idea of impurity in the Old Testament in the earlier books of the Law is employed in the later and more advanced ethical vocabulary of the Bible for a real sin against God as understood in the modern sense.

Again, we have other evidence besides the linguistic that the earliest conception of sin which we can call spiritual was still half-materialistic, and was still closely allied to that of bodily impurity. In the theory of earlier ritual, the sin can be washed away like a physical taint, the atonement takes the form of certain lustrations, and repentance is not considered necessary as a moral condition of release. And to the same middle stage of development belongs the process known as the transference of sin, whereby the sin can be extracted as if it were a substance from the person of the sinner and transferred into another man or animal or even an inanimate object. Think of sin as an inner vapour or exhalation and the idea of quasi-mechanical transference is intelligible.116.1 It no doubt belongs to a comparatively early period of savage religion. Among the Atkans, for instance,117.1 we hear of such a release as this: the sin, which in this case was a gross violation of a natural law of the sex-instinct, was made to enter into certain weeds which were worn about the person, and then, under a clear sun were carefully thrown away, the sun himself being called to witness the act of transference. In the ancient Peruvian Church, the shaking off of evils was a great public festival: bands of warriors marched forth crying out, "Go forth, all evils," and then bathed in the river, while the people shook out their clothes from the doors.117.2 A similar record speaks of the Inca praying to the river-god to bear away his sins, which he had confessed in the sight of the sun. And during the Peruvian purification a similar rule prevailed to that which was noticed above, that all abusive language and strife was to be avoided. Or again, the belief that the sin is an evil spirit that can be induced to find another living-lodgment, suggests the scapegoat, a familiar figure in Leviticus and in Greek ritual, the animal who bears away with it into the wilderness the sins of the people, or is put to death with the uttered prayer that into it may enter all the evils of the community. The Judaic record tells us that Aaron "confessed over him all the iniquities of the children of Israel...

putting them on the head of the goat"; after this, as the animal was in a high degree of sin-infection, both Aaron and the man who led it away into the wilderness must wash and change their clothes.118.1 The Egyptian rite described by Herodotus,118.2 shows us the same idea differently worked out: the head of the animal is severed with the imprecation that it may bear the evils of the community, and is then either thrown into the river so that the stream may carry them away, or is sold to the Hellenes wherever there happens to be a Hellenic market: Herodotus does not tell us the reason of this, which, however, is easily divined: the Hellene is the stranger who, as the Egyptians hoped, might eat the infected flesh and thereby absorb into his alien person the people's sins; for the eating of other people's sins is a recognised primitive process of transference.119.1 What is unique in the Egyptian management of the ceremony is the skilful combination of religion and trade.

Finally, the ritual may demand a human scapegoat, who will fulfil exactly the same function as the animal. He may be put to death, or driven over the border, carrying away the national sins: he may be very vile, and therefore a fitting receptacle for sin, like the "κάθαρμα," the "purifying man" in the Attic festival of the Thargelia, who was led through the streets, whipped with rods, and at one time burnt; or the slave at Marseilles,119.2 who was fed up and reverentially treated for a year, and then was led forth in solemn procession through the streets and expelled from the city, praying that on him might fall all the evils of the community:120.1 or the scapegoat-man may be exceptionally holy, being the better able, through his very holiness, to absorb harmlessly and dissipate the evils of others. Thus even the miserable victim of the Thargelia was mysteriously invested with a certain sacred character, and seems once to have been regarded in a certain degree as the counterpart of the divinity.120.2

Much of this ritual of sin-transference is altogether independent of the higher gods; it is worked by mesmeric or mimetic or mechanical magic. At a later period it is harmonised with their service and accompanied with prayer; and at this stage we note a curious ritualistic phenomenon. Blood, the primeval source of impurity, becomes itself a purifier, not by the law *similia similibus curantur*, but owing to the growing power of the sacrificial concept. "The blood of bulls and goats can wash away sins," because the animal that has been consecrated by contact with the altar becomes charged with a divine potency, and its sacred blood, poured over the impure man, absorbs and disperses his impurity. Illustrations are easily gathered from Hellenic ritual,121.1 which frequently employed the blood of swine for cathartic purposes. On an early vase-painting we see the hero Theseus seated on the altar of God the Atoner with pig's blood running down his body to cleanse him from the slaughter of the brigands.121.2 In the Judaic rule the blood of the red heifer was first sprinkled by the priest before the tabernacle of the congregation seven times, but for special purposes of lustration the "water of separation" was used, that is, water made holy by being mingled with the ashes of the heifer that had been burnt. We have a curious illustration of the double character of this water of separation: being consecrated and holy, it was powerful to cleanse away stain and sin: yet its own impure composition was not wholly forgotten, for he who sprinkled the water or touched it was unclean till evening.122.1

These ideas belong to very old-world thought, yet their reflex abides with us still in the heart of a spiritual creed; for their association is clear with the Christian conception of the transference of sin and of the divine victim that takes upon himself the sins of the people.

As far as we have examined it as yet, the concept of a "pure heart" is not necessarily wholly ethical; it is often coexistent with the ideas of sin that do not clearly recognise moral responsibility or the essential difference between deliberate wrong-doing and the ritualistic or accidental or involuntary sin. In the middle stage of ethical-religious growth, an innocent Œdipus may yet be regarded as πᾶς ἄναγνος, impure body and soul. The final point is reached when it is realised that the blood of bulls and goats cannot wash away sin, that nothing external can defile the heart or soul, but only evil thoughts and evil will. This purged and idealised concept will then in the progressive religions revolt against its own parentage, and will prompt the eternal antagonism of the prophet against the ritual priest, of the Christ against the Pharisee.

It would be interesting to trace the points of this long development, which has here been hastily sketched, among the higher races of the old world; but a brief and partial indication of its history among some of them must here suffice. We are all acquainted with the final evolution of the idea of purity in Judaic history: but the phenomena of its embryonic stages, as revealed in the ritual books of the Old Testament, may not be so familiar. They present the Hebrew mind in regard to this particular as on the same level with the Zarathustrian Persian, the Vedic Indian, and the Hellene of the seventh century. Purity is the strictest law of Jahvé, the pure god, who intimates that he would punish Aaron with death if he heedlessly entered the holy place without purification.124.1 But the processes by which it is secured are mechanical, quasi-magical, and the concept itself appears more materialistic than spiritual, ritualistic rather than ethical in our sense: the processes of cleansing are such as the use of incense, lustrations with blood, water, and even fire, cathartic methods which are almost universal: we hear nothing of prayer or repentance. Blood is the chief impurity, whether shed deliberately, accidentally, or righteously. The warriors after battle must be purified before they enter the camp.125.1 Murder has indeed become a tribal offence, and this marks a great advance in the social development of human society: no satisfaction such as the were-gilt was allowed for murder; but it is regarded as a sin rather than a crime, and its sinfulness is the uncleanness of the land on which the blood is shed. "Blood defileth the land," and "I the Lord dwell among the children of Israel."125.2 Even the accidental homicide must fly to the city of refuge, not merely to escape the avenger of blood, who represents the old family right of the blood-feud, but to rid the land of the impurity of his presence. Nor must he return till the death of the high priest.125.3 This latter restriction has not yet been explained, so far as I am aware. I venture the explanation that the high priest is regarded here as the temporary representative of Jahvé, and as infected with the impurity that cleaves to the outraged god; but when he dies, the stain that has been put upon the god fades away and his wrath ceases. Finally, we may note the rule that when the murderer could not be discovered, the nearest city must offer cathartic sacrifices, "and thy sin"—that is, the ritualistic sin of having an impure spot of ground in one's territory—"shall then be forgiven thee."126.1 In fact the Judaic law concerning homicide as shown in these books, though it has advanced far beyond savagery, and has even attained to the modern view that manslaying concerns the whole community, is yet barbaric on the whole. The concept of purity aided development up to a certain point and then probably retarded it. On the other hand, in the department of sexual morality its operation was most powerful for good; it consecrated and safeguarded the fundamental laws if it did not actually construct or evoke them; but, as we should expect, the sexual purity of the Hebrew code remains a religious law and does not pass into the domain of secular ethic.

Another religion that is of equal value for our present purpose is the Zarathustrian. Trusting as far as we may the translation and interpretation of its sacred books, we may gather the impression from the study of them that no religion on the earth has ever been under such bondage to the cathartic ideal as this one; nor does it appear very profitable at first sight to put the question here of the influence of the idea of purity on religion, law, and morals, for the idea seems all-absorbing and these three to have no independent existence apart from it. It creates for the Mazdean believer a morality of its own, with which the secular systems have little or nothing to do. "Oh, maker of the world," asks Zarathustra of Ahura Mazda, "can he be clean again who has eaten of the carcase of a dog or the corpse of a man?" The deity answers—"He cannot, oh holy Zarathustra."127.1 Nor is there any purification possible for the unforgivable sin of walking about after fifteen years of age were reached without a girdle or a proper shirt: "such a one goes henceforth with power to destroy the world of righteousness."128.1 On the other hand, the highest act of righteousness which brings forgiveness of all sins to him who performs it is the pulling down of a dakhma, the scaffold on which the corpses were hung according to the Persian system of burial, after it had served its purpose; for naturally it was a focus of impurity, and demons congregated there in swarms.128.2 And the Persian concept of purity makes its own law. As the ritual of cleansing is the prime article of the Zarathustrian code, so the sacrilegious cleanser, that is, the amateur who tried to purify another without knowledge of the Mazdean ceremonies, brought sterility upon the land and was punished with death.128.3 And death was the penalty for him who dared to carry a corpse alone, for the dead body spread around the contagion of a myriad "drugs" or demons, and two men at least must set hand to it to prevent an intolerable epidemic of impurity.129.1 Legislation in the Zend-Avesta is merciless beyond any recorded code; we must suppose that it was mainly idle thunder, or Persia would have been depopulated. The whole universe of Mazdeism is permeated with these cathartic ideas, and a secular or physical view of things scarcely glimmers through: the ritual order dominated what we call the material as well as the spiritual world; the sun, moon, and stars are purified by the Word. On this basis arose a religion of great exaltation and a religious fervour of rare intensity: and the sacred books of Persia are of great value for the present inquiry, for they show us more clearly than any other record the spiritual concept of the pure heart emerging from the ritualistic idea; while it is often hard in any particular text to distinguish between the lower and the higher significance. When God speaks to the prophet thus— "Purity is for man, next to life, the highest good: that purity, O Zarathustra, that is in the religion of Mazda for him who cleanses himself with good thoughts, words, and deeds,"130.1 we believe we have reached a high ethical conception; but the phrase is supposed by Darmesteter to refer to him who cleanses himself according to the prescriptions of the law. Yet in their cathartic code were the germs of an advanced morality, and truthfulness and chastity were fostered by it.130.2 The lustrations were partly of the primitive type, taken over, as usual, from a lower stratum of religion; their most interesting features are the cleansing words that accompanied them, which were not usually prayers but spells, formulæ of magic potency, but drawn from a high religion, such as these, for instance:—"The will of the Lord is the Law of Righteousness"; "Holiness is the best of all Good: it is also Happiness."131.1 Even the virtue of philanthropy is given cathartic value in a spell-formula, "he who relieves the poor makes Ahura King," recited before the person was washed with the holy water of Mazda and the "gômêz" of an ox.131.2

In a certain sense the Mazdean religion has been the "purest" the world has known; but the high spiritual concept of purity that it evolved never escaped nor struggled to escape, as did the Judaic and Hellenic, from the bondage to ritual. Therefore the religion was doomed to ceremoniousness and sacerdotalism; and the modern student who is fascinated with its frequent outbursts of genius and its deep, whole-hearted conviction must be prepared for the inevitable bathos that awaits him. Its remoteness from the modern and civilised view of things may be estimated from the Zarathustrian text, in which the prophet exalts the priestly medicine-man who heals the diseased limb with a cleansing spell and by the ejection of the demon, above the surgeon who heals it with a knife.132.1

It is with a feeling of relief that we now turn to the survey of the Hellenic phenomena, passing by as we must the Vedic and the Islamic, which appear to be of lesser importance so far as I have been able to study them. The Hellenic religion more than all others of the ancient world is the mirror of the manifold civilisation of a people; for its lesser intensity allowed it more varied application, and it was obliged to reconcile itself speedily with the utilitarian and secular forces of rational progress, which there was no sacerdotal caste strong enough to oppose. And it is in the light of this religion therefore that the concept of purity can best be studied in its relations to law and morality. The history of the cathartic ritual in Greece does not begin till the eighth century; for the Homeric age was strikingly sane, cheerful, and secular in its views about such things. Though Hektor feels, as any modern gentleman would feel, that it was wrong to go to a religious service "bedabbled in gore and filth," though Odysseus purifies his house with sulphur-fumigation after the carnage of the fight, the world for whom Homer sang does not appear to have been burdened with the ceremoniousness of purification or with dread of the impurity of blood and death, or with any sort of care for the vengeance or miasma of the ghost. An age that could rise to the height of such a sentiment as "best of omens is it to fight for one's country," was likely to be healthy-minded in all such matters. The first mention of purification for bloodshed is in a poem of Arctinos of the eighth century; and a certain ritual-code of purity begins to emerge in Hesiod. Henceforward cathartic legislation comes to be very rife in Greece, emanating chiefly from two centres as it seems, Delphi and Crete. The gods to whom the domain of ritual-purity belongs especially are Apollo, Zeus, and Dionysos; at the same time the ghostly terrors of the underworld appear to be gaining a greater hold on the Hellenic imagination, and "catharsis" is specially needed to deal with these. Probably all this is only a revival of aboriginal practices and superstitions rooted in the Hellenic soil, a religion which the intellectualism of Homeric civilisation had happily suppressed for a time, but which asserted itself with renewed strength when that civilisation was overthrown. Yet the revival, though apparently a "set-back," bore fair fruit for morality, law, and even religion. The history of Greek ethic must reckon as it has not yet done with the ritual of purity, and the history of Greek law with the fear of the ghost and the miasma of bloodshed.

At first the idea is, as usual, ritualistic and non-moral: and much that we find in savage communities, and in Judæa, Persia, and India, we find again in Greece. As the Hebrew warriors were purified before returning to camp, so the Macedonian army was purified in spring before the campaign,135.1 and the misunderstood story of the Phokians daubing themselves with gypsum before battle points to a cathartic ritual.135.2 And the Hellenic ceremonies agreed with those of most other nations in regard to the causes of uncleanness and the methods of deliverance: fire, water, blood, onions, the skins of animals sacrificed, even clay and bran, are the usual purifying media. In one method of κάθαρσις only the Hellenic ritual is unique so far as I know: sacrificial communion with God was sometimes considered an effective means of obliterating the impurity which the kinsmen contracted by a death in the family: at Argos the mourners put off the "tapu" by eating of the sacrifice to Apollo, believing that the spirit of the pure god in the sacred food could destroy the miasma within and around them.136.1 The strongholds of Pharisaic purification were the religious brotherhoods of Orphism and the earlier Pythagoreanism, a religious-philosophic school closely associated with the former; in these the law of "the pure life" is a ceremonious law, specially concerned with abstinence from certain food. But Greek thought did not remain long on this level: a saying is attributed to Charondas of Catana, but perhaps of later origin, which asserts that "foul speech is a defilement of the soul";136.2 and in a fragment of Epicharmos of the fifth century, we have the utterance of the higher gospel, "If thou art pure of soul, thou art pure of all thy body"; and the later Pythagorean literature, such as the "Golden Song" of Hierocles, contains the doctrine that "purity of soul is the only divine service"; "God has no more familiar abode on the earth than the pure soul." And to an unknown writer, probably of the same school,137.1 we owe the dogma, "We worship God most meetly if we render our own soul pure from every stain of evil." There are two epigrams in the Anthology, included in the fanciful collection of Pythian oracles, expressing the same idea that holiness is a spiritual fact independent of ceremonies or lustrations: "Oh stranger, if holy of soul, enter the shrine of the holy God, having but touched the lustral water: lustration is an easy matter for the good, but all ocean with its streams cannot cleanse the evil man."137.2 The other maintains as clearly as Isaiah or the New Testament the uselessness of all mere washing of hands: "The temples of the gods are open to all good men, nor is there any need of purification: no stain can ever cleave to virtue. But depart, whosoever is baneful at heart, for thy soul will never be washed by the cleansing of the body."137.3 The better Greek mind attained this freedom the more easily in that it was not strongly or generally possessed with the belief in the aboriginal impurity or sinfulness of the flesh and the earthly life. And Greek ritual itself, conservative as it was and never abandoning its code of purification, comes at last to be influenced by this freer atmosphere and to reconcile ceremonious purity with a higher moral law. Before the temple of Asclepios at Epidauros stood the text, "Within the incense-filled sanctuary one must be pure; and purity is to have righteous thoughts."138.1 An inscription on a temple in Rhodes of the time of Hadrian138.2 shows a strange blend of primitive and advanced thought. Its preamble mentions "rules concerning righteous entrance into the shrine." "The first and greatest rule is to be pure and unblemished in hand and heart and to be free from an evil conscience." Then follows the usual ceremonious code of rules concerning the impurities of food, funerals, and natural affections of the body: and the last clause shows the ethical idea penetrating even these, for the code prescribes that a person may enter the shrine "on the same day after lawful married intercourse." This means that the adulteress was excluded, as she was at Athens by a law quoted by Demosthenes.139.1 It appears then that the liberal ethic judgment attributed to Theano, the female Pythagorean teacher, that while lawful intercourse was no bar to participating in a religious service on the same day, the adulteress was to be for ever excluded,139.2 was not wholly out of accordance with the advanced ritualistic code of Greece.

The above is some slight illustration of the development of the Greek concept of purity and of its ethical influence. It remains to trace its action in a very important department of law — the law of homicide. Perhaps the most significant distinction between the code of a civilised and that of a savage or barbaric community lies in their respective attitudes towards manslaughter or murder: in the latter society it is mainly an affair between the families concerned, to be settled by the were-gilt or the blood-feud: in the former the whole community feels itself to be deeply concerned. Our Teutonic ancestors, at the time of Tacitus and for centuries after, remained at the lower stage, though we discern that the legal genius of the Icelanders was impelling them towards the higher even before Christianity reached them. What is strange is that some societies appear to have attained a high general level of civilisation without making this momentous advance: the Homeric world, for instance, was scarcely abreast with the early Icelandic in this respect, although we may see signs that the higher idea was ready to emerge in the later Homeric period.140.1 Then follows a blank in our record which may be tentatively filled up by the interpretation of mythology, until in the developed Attic law—which we know better than the law of any other Greek state—we find the modern idea fully recognised and applied to a criminal code, probably from the sixth century onward, though traces of legal barbarism still survive. We would gladly discover the constructive forces, spiritual or political, that brought this great reform about. The anthropology of our contemporary savage societies has not yet supplied us with analogies that we could apply to Greek history: a few savage states have indeed spontaneously achieved the great advance from the blood-feud to a public law of homicide, but there is no record showing how they have achieved it. Some writers have supposed that the emergence of criminal law in general is always due to some great increase of power in the central government, probably to the development of the monarchy. But as a universal axiom this cannot be accepted; for, as Steinmetz in his treatise on "The Development of Punishment"142.1 has shown, such a suggested cause is not found operative in the backward communities of modern times that have developed a public criminal law. Nor would it be reasonable to urge that the central authority was stronger in Greece of the seventh century than in the earlier monarchical period. Probably Steinmetz is right in his belief that among savage societies the earliest criminal law arises from some intense feeling of hatred or dread excited by acts that violate religious feeling or secular interests. One of the earliest crimes to be punished by death at the hands of the society is incest: the horror that it excites among savages is a feeling that we may call religious. We may not be able to show indeed that the primitive ideas of purity would explain the earliest complicated codes of human marriage: but the circles of kinship that are thus established seem certainly to have been consecrated at a very early time by the concept of purity that came to be attached to them.143.1 Now it is probable that a similar religious feeling was operative in the case of homicide.

If in any given society the primitive belief in the impurity of bloodshed became intensified beyond a certain point, homicide might easily come to be regarded no longer as a matter to be settled by the families of the slayer and the slain, but as the deep concern of the people of the land. We have seen that it was just this religious concept of impurity that brought the act under the cognisance of the national religious law of Israel: the people are terrified because the soil has been made impure and their god has been stained. In the Zend-Avesta we find that the slaying of a water-dog was an impure act against God, and was avenged by the whole community; and sacrifice was offered to appease the holy soul of the dog.144.1 These facts then offer some analogy for the theory that I would suggest, namely, that the civilised law in Greece concerning homicide arose in the post-Homeric period through an intensification of the feeling concerning the impurity of bloodshed and owing to the greater hold that the terrors of the ghostly world had come to gain over the later Hellenic imagination; for the ghost or the Erinys of the dead is the embodiment of the miasma that arises from the slaying; and the ghost knows how to drive it home, and is no respecter of persons, but can make a whole area uninhabitable. The religious phenomenon and the legal fact that I would connect as cause and effect are not found in the Homeric period: both are found coexisting in the later. And much legendary evidence accords with this hypothesis. Perhaps the earliest indication of the emergence of the idea in Greek society that certain kinds of homicide concern the State, is found in the legends about exile and excommunication for the shedding of kindred blood, the exile, for instance, of Bellerophon and Ixion. Such exile is not the ordinary flight of the homicide to avoid the avenger of blood; for in the cases where a man is of the same kin as the slain, there is no family avenger, but the whole community in horror cast him out lest the curse should infect themselves. Kinsmen's blood was more sacred than other, therefore the shedding it spread the greater impurity over the land. And the Greek legends suggest that this offence was one of the earliest in the legal history of the race which awoke the religious conscience of the State.145.1 Now if we assume that the old ideas associated with kinship came to be extended to the whole community of the polis—as might easily happen through the intermarriage of the γένη—then a similar miasma would be caused by the slaying of a citizen as by kindred murder: the State would feel the supernatural peril of the act and would take cognisance.

The reasons for supposing that this was the actual order in the Hellenic evolution of the homicide law may appear to rest on mere legends, but legends are often direct and firsthand evidence of early thought, and the stories about the slayers of kindred who were driven out of the communities and who were the first applicants for the ritual of purification, such as Ixion, Orestes, Theseus, accord well with the early belief that the Erinyes were the ghostly avengers of kindred slaughter. Then we find that in the Aithiopis, the poem of Arctinos of Miletus, Achilles has to leave the army and retire to Lesbos for purification, although Thersites, whom he has slain, is no real kinsman of his: whence we may draw the conclusion that the State of Miletus, in the eighth century, had come to take cognisance of the slaying of any citizen. And the Argives, in the fifth or fourth century, offer atonement to Zeus Meilichios for a civic massacre, the god who has a legendary association with purification for the shedding of kindred blood. By the fifth century in Athens the religious feeling concerning the sacredness of all life within the city had so deepened that even the slaying of a slave caused a miasma and was a State offence.147.1

Now when we examine certain details of Attic law, together with certain expressions of sentiment concerning homicide in the classical writers of Attica, we see the clear imprint of its origin. Accidental homicide was as gravely regarded by the Athens of the fourth century as by the old Hebrew code: such homicides must fly over the border, but if they went by a certain road, the State refused to allow the avenger of blood to follow them: they must remain in exile until they have won the forgiveness of one of the kinsmen of the dead.148.1 We may suppose that the kinsmen are regarded as taking up the feud of the ghost, who is likely to be vindictive, even when the slaying was accidental. Finally, when the pardoned homicide returns he must go through elaborate purifications. These latter were to wipe off the miasma, not to ease what we might call the burden of conscience. And the community were obliged to expel temporarily even a perfectly innocent man, because of their fear of the wrath of the dead. This dread of the ghost is appealed to by an Attic orator as a motive that should influence the judges to condemn the prisoner.148.2 The first legal preliminary in a case of murder, which reveals clearly the religious origin of the State law, was the solemn proclamation, made by one of the relatives holding a spear at the funeral, that the murderer should keep aloof from all the holy and public places of the community. And Antiphon strongly expresses the popular sentiment that the unpunished murderer pollutes the public altars and vitiates the atmosphere of the city: and the whole of Plato's legislation149.3 concerning homicide is based on the idea of the miasma arising from bloodshed, and is quite in accord with Attic law. The exile of the murderer purges the city as well as his execution; therefore the accused was allowed to go out of the country before the verdict.149.4 The contagion was worse under a roof than in the open air; therefore the Athenian judges insisted on trying homicide in an unroofed court, "lest they should be under one roof with the slayer."149.5 Also it is part of primitive animistic belief that such miasma could cleave to things which had caused the death of a man: hence the inanimate object such as an axe or bar of iron might be solemnly tried and, if found guilty, would be thrown into the sea to rid the State of infection:150.1 the same superstition explains the old English law that a waggon which ran over a man and caused his death should be given to God—"deodand": that is, it was to become a perquisite of the King, who represented God.

So far we seem to discern clearly the concept of purity evolving State law in a very vital matter. And this is a great achievement. But it might easily evolve law which from our point of view would be unjust and superstitious. The terrors of the ghost, the inequitable wrath of a pure god, the insistence on the ritualistic view of impurity, might retard progress and prevent the evolution of the highest law which regards extenuating circumstances and admits justifiable homicide. Such law is not heard of in the Mosaic books, but it existed in the Attic code,151.1 which specially on this account may be called civilised. The court which tried admitted cases of homicide where the plea of justification was raised was the Delphinion, and its foundation legend claimed that it was instituted to try Theseus for slaying the Pallantids who attacked him, and that the plea of justifiable homicide was allowed.151.2 The name of the court shows that its patron is the pure god, and points to Crete and Delphi, the chief centres of the ritual of purification. Now it is quite possible that this momentous advance in law may have been prompted by the healthy rationalism of the early Greek mind, to some extent by secular utilitarian thought, which reacted on the religious view of purity. We shall then say that the religion adapted itself dexterously to a secular movement, as it usually did in Greece. Or it may be the truth that the advance was due to a spontaneous movement within the religion itself, beginning perhaps in the seventh century, and to the growing consciousness that the purity or impurity of an act depended on motive and will. If this idea penetrated at an early time, as it certainly did at a later, into the sacerdotal circle, then the priest of Apollo might grant or withhold purification according to the degree of justification the homicide might prove:152.1 in this case a court would be established at the instigation of the purifying god to consider the circumstances. This explanation must remain a hypothesis, but it is one that assumes the action of real forces.

Enough has been said to illustrate the intimate association of the idea of purity with legal progress,152.2 and it only remains to indicate very briefly its impress and effect on religious institutions. One of the methods most frequently employed to attain mental purity or freedom from the evil spirit is fasting; from all human societies, primitive and advanced, we could gather a copious stock of illustration. And mankind has, on the whole, agreed as to the occasions at which the ritual is desirable; in spring before the crops and the first-fruits appear, before the warriors go forth to battle, before any kind of intimate communion with God, when the family is in mourning for a kinsman and evil influences are abroad, fasting has been practised as a mode of purging the body and safeguarding it against spiritual harm or preparing it for the privilege of divine intercourse. It has been held necessary before any mystic initiation,154.1 the early Christian Church prescribing it for the days preceding the Easter communion; also before the individual can attain the divine afflatus of prophecy or the supernatural potency for expelling evil spirits or working wonder-cures. "Such kind goeth not forth save by prayer and fasting." The psychological basis of the ritual is the belief that certain foods, and finally all food, are liable to engender evil influences in the body; and, moreover, the experience that the abstinence generates a peculiar mental condition of exaltation, ecstasy, and supra-normal self-confidence: other ideas, such as the discipline of self-denial, that come to gather round the practice are of later growth.

From the same primitive view of the relations between our body and the spiritual world has arisen the enforcement of celibacy upon the priesthood. To trace the phenomenon, which is commonly or exceptionally found in all human societies, throughout the history of the churches, would require a separate chapter. It is not a late growth in religion, nor of necessity a sign of high development. And here again the original psychological motive is not a spirit of self-mortification, but the belief that the chaste body is the purer abode for the Divine Spirit, and the mental experience that such self-abnegation usually engenders a stronger consciousness of religious power. There are signs that the idea is losing its hold on the modern consciousness, but we see the deep impress it has made upon some of the ideas and dogmas of our religion. The institution of a sacerdotal rule of celibacy corresponds to the view prevalent in any given society of the priestly function; it is likely to be enforced when the priest is invested with a specially prophetic and mystic character, and is required to mediate between the society and God by means of frequent communion with the divinity: it is rare when the civic and semi-secular view of the sacerdotal office prevails, rare therefore among the Northern Aryans and in the pre-Christian Greek and Roman states, although the Hellenic ritual generally required virginity, or at least a prolonged chastity, in the prophetess and occasionally in the ordinary priest. It was common in the ecstatic religions of Anatolia, and in the worship of Cybele was pushed to an unnatural extreme. It is interesting again to trace the association between the Phrygian-Christian heresy of Montanism and the older Phrygian paganism; and we have noted that Montanus, its founder, the champion of celibacy, is reported to have been in his unconverted days a priest of Cybele.

Again, the baptismal rite is a form of purification of world-wide prevalence, as has been already intimated. The washing of the new-born has been generally interpreted as a purgation of dangerous and evil influence among the lower as well as the higher races. An interesting form of such lustration is recorded of the old Aztec home-life: the midwife washed the infant with the prayer, "May this water purify and whiten thy heart: may it wash away all that is evil."157.1 The adult, before initiation into any mystic society, usually needed elaborate purification; and this often took the form of baptism with water and occasionally with blood: and in certain of the Mediterranean religions the lustration was not merely regarded as a washing away of the old sin, but as a spiritual rebirth.157.2 In the Isis rites the baptism with water was supposed to raise the mortal to the divinity: in the description of the baptismal purification of Setis I. the words occur: "I have purified thee with life and power, so as to make thee young, like thy father Ra." And the gods themselves were believed to be reborn through the sprinkling of lustral water over their images.157.3 We discover the same theories held by the early Church concerning the Christian rite: the font washes away the taint of the flesh, while at the same time the divine potency of the water revivifies and recreates the catechumen, who dies to the old life and is born again; so that the font, which itself was exorcised and purified in the early period, was in some sense the womb of spiritual life, and the rite is both an exorcism and a communion. Very soon in the history of the Church it came to be regarded as of such serious and critical significance that the catechumen must prepare himself for it by prior purifications and exorcisms: such ceremonies as the breathing on his forehead by the priest, the sacramental partaking of the salt, the anointing with oil, together with the utterance of a prayer that "the enemy might be put to flight," have an obvious cathartic significance.158.1

We must also regard confession as a kind of purification; for the "speaking out" of sin would be regarded as a real purgation and deliverance at that period of thought when words might be viewed as things, or at least as controlling things. This was its meaning in the preliminary ritual of the Samothracian Mysteries, in the Mexican religion159.1 where it was associated with purification and the concept of rebirth, and finally in the early Christian Church, where it was specially imposed upon the priest before the Easter communion as part of the purificatory preparation.159.2 An interesting formula of confession is found among the Babylonian liturgical tablets: the penitent prays to the god and the goddess—"Let the seven winds carry away my sighs… let the bird bear my wickedness to the heavens: let the fish carry off my misery, let the river sweep it away. Let the beast of the field take it from me. Let the waters of the river wash me clean." Here the purificatory confessional works partly by prayer to the high god, partly by the old idea of the magic transference of sin into an alien substance.160.1

These are examples of practices in the advanced religions aiming at the purging of internal and spiritual sin. But the older and more materialistic view of impurity as a physical taint or as the miasma of an evil spirit, has not wholly faded even from historic Christianity: the ceremony of the churching of women, though transformed into a thanksgiving service, has descended from an old cathartic ritual that purged away the dangerous pollution of child-birth: and the consecration of churches was originally merely a special application of the old-world practice of purifying the house against demons, as we may see from the legendary example given in the apocryphal "Acts of St Thomas."160.2

The facts which I have collected and exposed, incomplete as the statement is, may justify what was said at the outset of the inquiry, that the aboriginal idea of purity has struck deep roots in the soil on which much of our ethical thought and feeling, many of our legal and religious institutions, have grown and developed. The concept, owing perhaps to its immemorial continuity of life and deep primeval instinctiveness, if the word may pass, is liable to fantastic exaggerations. It has sometimes proved itself an insurmountable barrier to moral and legal progress. When it has crystallised into a hard "pharisaic" form, it has arrested and imprisoned the life of a hitherto progressive people. On the other hand, though its innate quality, so to speak, is never secular-utilitarian, its contributions to our civilisation have been, as we have seen, of inestimable service. It has engendered the modern horror of murder and bloodshed, and the ideal of the chaste life: we owe to it in great degree the delicate sensitiveness of spiritually gifted characters. For good and for evil, it has been an instinctive religious force more potent than any other of these in the mental evolution of man.

LECTURE IV
THE EVOLUTION OF PRAYER FROM LOWER TO HIGHER FORMS

There is no part of the religious service of mankind that so clearly reveals the various views of the divine nature held by the different races at the different stages of their development as the formulæ of prayer, or reflects so vividly the material and psychologic history of man. The historic material at our disposal is unfortunately modern, not reaching back, that is to say, to a period earlier than some four thousand years before Christ; but this can be supplemented, as usually happens, by the evidence gathered from the lower societies, as well as by the observation of practices that frequently accompany and are very closely blended with prayer even in the higher religions, and that we may with confidence believe to have descended from an immemorial antiquity. The question as to the origin of prayer is one of great difficulty and of the deepest significance for the history and philosophy of religion; for it inevitably involves the questions concerning the origin of the belief in a personal divinity, concerning the relation of magic to religion, of the spell-ritual which commands or constrains to a prayer-ritual of humiliation and entreaty. Even if I had an original and matured judgment to put before you on questions of such importance, a single lecture would be a very inadequate space for its exposition.164.1 Therefore, though I may indicate, I will not attempt in this lecture to decide on, the question of origin. I will content myself with arranging the phenomena according as they appear from our point of view to belong to a lower stratum of religion or a higher; such an arrangement begs no question, and agrees with our experience that in all religions, whether savage or civilised, lower and higher elements are able to coexist. I will first give a general sketch of the facts, with some interpretation of them, and will follow this with an illustrative selection of the prayers of primitive and advanced communities.

According to the modern definition of prayer, man addresses uttered or inaudible speech to a divine power conceived as Spirit or God, but always as personal, in order to obtain material, moral, or spiritual blessings: that part of the address that contains the actual prayer will be often accompanied by words of homage, adoration, confession of sin, expressions of doctrinal faith, statements concerning the beneficent operations of the divinity in time past, self-assuring utterances of confidence in divine protection or the divine promise. Though the formulæ contain much positive statement and are by no means confined to the optative mood, the attitude of the supplicator is always reverential and self-abased; modern religion reprobates any idea of compelling the divinity; only it generally seals its petitions with the mystic signature of a powerful name. If this may pass as a fairly comprehensive and adequate account of modern or advanced prayer, it will still be found to contain elements that may descend from a very ancient mould of religious thought not easy to reconcile with our higher religious consciousness; and it is no adequate account of the various modes which less advanced societies have used and are still using to express their desires to the supernatural power. It has indeed been recently asserted, with some plausibility,166.1 that no savage community yet explored lacks the conception of a high god making for righteousness; and certainly many of the lower races have spontaneously developed genuine prayer in the modern sense. Still it is sometimes reported by scientific observers that some backward peoples do not pray at all;167.1 and it appears not to be uncommon for the savage to regard his high god as too remote to be addressed for any practical purpose.

But the savage, though he may pray as we do, has other ways of addressing himself to the unseen personal agencies that he believes to surround him; and these are the ways of magic and the magic-spell. Having learned from human experience that he can project his will-power by an occult process so as to subdue the mind of his fellow-man, he experiments with this method upon the world of nature and spirits: he deals with ghosts chiefly in this way, though he may pray to them also; and he has no reluctance in applying his magic even to the higher divinities. As magic-worker he stands on a different footing altogether from the petitioner: his attitude towards the supernatural power is self-confident and imperious, his speech is no prayer but a command. He may project his will by dumb show, by action suggestive of his desire: but in most cases he will probably prefer to accompany it with potent speech, so as to drive his will home to the mark, so to speak: and the psychology of such magic practices has been ably investigated by recent writers. The technical name for such exercise of will upon another person is suggestion; a modern application of it sometimes appears in the extreme form that we call mesmerism or hypnotism. For the successful application of the charm, it is often an essential condition that one should possess oneself of the name of the person against whom it is directed, and at times of his picture or effigy, for both the name and the picture are regarded as vital parts of the whole individuality that one seeks to control. The same ideas transferred into the world of supernatural personalities account for the potency and deep significance that attaches to the divine name, and for the prominence of the picture and the effigy in the religious magic. But the savage has also learned from experience that he can work upon his fellows by entreaty, flattery, soothing and endearing address: and it was obviously natural for him to approach the divine powers in the same fashion, and to use humble and prayerful petitions. Nor does there seem any reason why he should not employ the methods of magic and prayer simultaneously or in close conjunction on the same occasion. We may often in fact be in doubt whether to interpret a certain primitive religious act from one point of view or the other. Thus we are told that when the Khonds of Orissa are about to enter on a campaign, "the priest cuts a branch and dresses it and arms it, so as to personate one of the foe: thereupon it is thrown down at the shrine of the war-god":169.1 This formal appeal to the god is speechless, and may be thought to be a speechless prayer; but it is of the same colour as a multifarious mass of practices which are mimetic and which are intended to work by means of suggestion. A singular ritual is recorded of the rain societies of North America:170.1 emblems or picture-writing representing clouds, with vertical drops symbolising rain, are placed on an altar, ears of maize are placed by the side of them with other objects, and the corn-ears are sprinkled with water, while at the same time prayers are proffered to the ghosts that control the rain-supply. We would wish to know what the manner of the praying is; but it seems clear that we here have the ritual of prayer combined with magic-suggestion, which consists in pretending to do the thing which it is desired to bring about. Again, the primitive formulæ devised to drive out the demons of disease and poverty are usually imperious commands and not prayers: such as the Chinese "Let the devil of poverty depart";170.2 the Greek, "Go out, hunger,"170.3 and "To the door, you ghosts."170.4

But when, as in Buro, the bidding takes such a form as "Grandfather small-pox, go away,"171.1 the reverential and soothing address allows us to approximate this to prayer, for in the liturgies of the earlier as well as the advanced religions the divinity is commonly addressed in terms of kinship. We shall note instances of real prayers proffered by the uncultured races to a high god, yet retaining something of the magic character and tone: we detect it in the mystic employment of the name, in the reiteration of the same short phrase, in the droning sing-song in which, according to Professor Tylor,171.2 savage prayers are usually intoned, the tone of a mesmeric incantation. But gradually, as the concept of divinity deepens in the progressive race, and the mind becomes penetrated with the consciousness of the littleness of man and of the incomparable greatness of God, the worshipper tends to become the humble petitioner and prayer comes to predominate over spell.

And it has happened in the legislation of the higher religions that magic at last becomes "suspect" and tabooed: yet the most austere and purified religion often unconsciously retains certain elements of spell-ritual, and even legitimatises the spell by virtue of the distinction between white magic and black. The distinction is morphologically unsound, and arises generally from *ex-parte* prejudice. We do not find, in fact, if we broadly compare the phenomena of all religions, that cleavage and irreconcilable antagonism between magic and religion which has often been supposed. Even in religions that we must class as high, the deity himself is often imagined to work by means of magic, and the Christian Church itself has given its patronage and consecration to practices of magical significance, such as the ordeal, purification, certain forms of healing, exorcisms of evil spirits: all these will be accompanied by prayers to God, but the prayers are so impregnated with the ideas of animistic magic that we can hardly regard them as pure forms. Nevertheless, though the lower elements are so difficult to eradicate, yet the experience of some few of the higher communities may reassure us that as a religion progresses in spirituality it can purge itself more and more thoroughly of these, and the progress is from spell to prayer.

Again, we may compare the phenomena from the point of view of the progress in aspiration. In the primitive period, when the struggle is to live at all rather than to live well, the objects of prayer must be material blessings, and these are still prominent in the liturgies of the civilised societies. There is a sameness in all these, and the chief distinction to note is between the prayers that look to the individual alone and those that look to the good of the community. A higher stage is reached when moral and spiritual qualities become the object of prayer; and when this is attained, the principle of prayer is likely to become more and more spiritual, and the petitioner more and more diffident in the expression of his material wants, and with a growing consciousness that the Deity knows best what is good for man, may rise to the height of the formula, "Thy will be done." It is interesting to note in how many races some such utterance has been heard; and at times men may have been helped to it by the consciousness which scientific advance had awakened, that the laws of the material universe cannot be capriciously altered to suit the temporary needs of the individual: a formula of acquiescence appears then to be the deepest and truest prayer. Finally, in the evolution of prayer we may consider that the consummation is marked by the theory, maintained by later Greek philosophy and early Christian fathers alike, that the true intention of prayer is not the mere petition for some special blessing, but rather the communion with God, to whom it is a spiritual approach. Here as often elsewhere, the highest spiritual product of human thought reveals its affinity with some dimly remote primeval concept; for much of the spell-ritual at which we have been glancing implies an idea of such communion, the human agent endeavouring to charge himself with a potency drawn from a quasi-divine source.

It remains now to take concrete examples from the record of prayer illustrative of these phases of development. Looking first at the savage races, we have already observed that some of their formulæ seem to belong to the borderland between spell and prayer. When the New Caledonian says over the fire that he kindles to increase the heat of the sun, "Sun, I do this that you may be burning hot," it is obviously not a prayer that he utters to the sun-god but a formula expressing the suggestion of his magic.175.1 And when the Karens of Burma at the threshing of the rice call out to the corn-mother, "Shake thyself, grandmother, shake thyself. Let the paddy ascend till it equals a hill, equals a mountain; shake thyself, grandmother, shake thyself,"176.1 we have surely a command rather than a pure prayer; for primitive vegetation-ritual works by compulsion rather than entreaty. On the other hand, we have record of a genuine Karen prayer addressed to "the God of heaven and earth, God of the mountains and hills," on the occasion when a sin of unchastity was supposed to have sterilised the earth: "Do not be angry with me, do not hate me, but have mercy on me and compassionate me…. Now I repair the mountains, now I heal the hills…. Make thy paddy fruitful, thy rice abundant…. If we cultivate but little, still grant that we may obtain a little." But the prayer is accompanied with rites that are purely magical and aiming at the restoration of the earth.176.2

The buffalo clan among the Sioux Indians decorate themselves with emblems of their totem animal before going on the war-path, and express the purpose of the dressing with a sententious phrase: "My little grandfather is always dangerous when he makes an attempt."177.1 Such an utterance, considered formally, is not a prayer but a statement about the power of the buffalo, "the little grandfather"; for it is an article of faith in the magic creed that the supernatural force, which the spell aims at setting in operation, can be made to work by definite statements that it is working; these are suggestive assurances that increase one's own confidence; and the Sioux formula is of such a nature; only the coaxing and endearing phrase of kinship seems to imply a half entreaty as well. We discern more clearly the rudiments of a prayer in the words addressed by the Santee Indians to the buffalo when they have offered him a feast: "Grandfather, venerable man, thy children have made this feast for you: may the food thus taken cause them to live and bring them good fortune."178.1 The account of the Sioux religion preserves a quaint form of words which are used for the riddance of the ghost, to despatch the soul of the deceased to the home of the dead: "You are going to the animals, you are going to your ancestors, you came hither from the animals and you are going back thither: do not face this way again: when you go, continue walking."178.2 The tone of the words is kind and considerate, but authoritative rather than supplicatory, and unlike the formula which the same Indians are reported to use when praying to their ancestors for good weather or good hunting, "Spirits of the dead, have mercy on us."178.3 Certain prayers used habitually by the Todas of the Nalgiri hills for the thriving of the dairy and the buffalo herd have recently been published,178.4 and as the formulæ are all in the optative mood—"May it be well for the buffaloes, may there be no destroyer, etc.," and there is an appeal to divine personages or powers—"for the sake of such or such a god may this happen"—we may class them as prayers; but the appeal is very faint and the formulæ seem to be used as if they possessed a self-dependent efficacy. More interesting and fervent is the address to the sun, proffered by a solitary hunter of the half-christianised Kekchi tribe of Indians:179.1 his object is to secure game and food in the wilderness both for himself and as an oblation to the god; but in the very long and impassioned utterance, with its many repetitions, there is very little direct entreaty: the Indian contents himself with definite and reassuring statements concerning the omnipresence of the deity and the ease with which the latter can execute his will: "It will give you no trouble to give me all kind of game"; and a moving appeal is made on the ground of kinship: "Thou art my father: who is my mother, who is my father? Only thou, O God."

We may regard these utterances of the hunter not indeed as spells, for his attitude is most reverent and loving, but as potent statement effecting the purpose of prayer. Nor need we see Christian influence in the striking phrase last quoted, though of course this is possible; such endearing address is common both in the lower and higher liturgies. the Egyptian appealed to Isis in similar terms180.1 —"Oh my father, my brother, my mother Isis," the Babylonian addressed Bel as father and mother,180.2 and a Vedic hymn contains the phrase, "Thou, oh Agni, art our father, we are thy kinsmen."180.3 Such appeals, suggested by the affection between kinsmen and the idea of the kinship of man with God, belong to the alphabet of pure prayer.

Of still more value for the light it throws on the attitude of the Indian's mind to the powers of the unseen world, is the so-called prayer of a Navajo Shaman belonging to the district of Arizona, recently published in the *American Anthropologist*;181.1 and to understand it the circumstances must be briefly stated. The Shaman had been telling the American inquirer the story of his tribe's descent through the lower world and their re-emergence: after the narrative he fears that speaking about the lower regions may have caused his own spiritual or astral part to have left his body and departed thither; and he therefore proceeds to recite a long so-called prayer intended to deliver his soul from the witchcraft that may be detaining it below. We should not strictly call it a prayer at all, but a narrative in the indicative mood stating that the war-gods of the tribe are actually doing what he specially wants them to do, namely, to go down and rescue his soul from the woman-chieftain, "the underground witch." Every step of their way there and back is carefully recounted several times over, so that they cannot go wrong; and when they are supposed to have brought back his soul, the recital ends with the joyful refrain, "The world before me is restored in beauty: my voice is restored in beauty," each phrase repeated five times. It is really a spell-narrative about the gods, having the same effect as prayer, and is a twofold illustration of the primitive idea that talking about a thing makes it happen; an idea not wholly extinct among ourselves, and possibly underlying some of the liturgies of higher religions.

For the rest, savages often pray very much as the civilised man, and accompany some of their purifications and medicine-magic with real prayers to higher gods to give them efficacy: for instance, the African doctor administering the medicine shown him by the fetich holds it first up to heaven and prays, "Father Heaven, bless this medicine that I now give."183.1 But I have not been able to find any example of a savage prayer for moral or spiritual blessings. An interesting feature is, however, observable in a verbose and very exacting prayer made by the Khonds of Orissa to the earth-goddess; after particularising very carefully their material wants, they conclude with the words, "We are ignorant of what it is good to ask for. You know what is good for us, give it us."183.2 This appears to be a unique savage version of the great phrase, "Thy will be done."

Turning now to the liturgies of the more advanced peoples,183.3 we may note briefly at the outset one feature that is found in most of them if not common to all; namely, the idea that the prayer gains potency from the solemn utterance of the true divine name. The phenomenon has been examined by recent writers on comparative religion, especially by Giesebrecht in his treatise on *Die Alt-testamentliche Schätzung des Gottesnamens*.184.1 In primitive psychology, the name is part of the personality, and the soul or power of the individual inheres in it: therefore he who has the name of the person, whether human, superhuman, or divine, can exercise a certain control over him by means of its magical application. Thus in the appeal to the god Ukko in the Kalevala, "Ukko, oh thou god in heaven, Ukko come, we call upon thee, Ukko come, we need thee sorely," there is virtue in the threefold repetition of the name, and the passage is part of an address which is called "magic words." Evidence from Teutonic paganism, so far as I know, is lacking, although the idea has left its clear imprint on the human saga.

Its influence is strongest and its operation most interesting in the liturgies of the Mediterranean and of India. In old Latium, it seems, the pontifices endeavoured to conceal the true names of the gods, lest they might be wrongly used by unauthorised persons185.1 or lest the enemy should get the knowledge of them and therewith the power to draw the divinities away. We may thus understand the often misinterpreted statement in Herodotus, that the Pelasgian deities were nameless; and the Greeks themselves must have been familiar with the ritual precaution of keeping secret the divine name, as we may gather from the phrase in the Euripidean fragment185.2 about the enlightened man "who knows the silent names of the gods": it is curious to find exactly the same expression in a Vedic hymn,185.3 in which the sacrificial post, or tree to which the sacrifices were attached, is thus addressed: "Where thou knowest, oh tree, the sacred names of the gods, to that place make the offerings go." It is possible that the same superstition may have been the original cause of the custom that has sometimes been observed of silent or inaudible prayer: the formulæ with the divine name attached to them being of such potency that they must be concealed.

The belief that the name belongs to the essence of the personality explains the curious formula in the Umbrian prayer preserved in the Tabulæ Iguvinæ, where the god Grabovius is implored to be propitious to the "Arx Fisia" and to "the name of the Arx Fisia," as if the name of the city was a living and independent entity.

In the Greek liturgies we note the anxious care with which particular qualifying epithets were selected and attached to the personal name of the divinity, so as to make clear what was the precise operation of divine favour which the prayer aimed at evoking. This explains why so many divinities, some of whom were scarcely known outside a narrow area, were invoked as πολυώνυμε, "thou god of many names," all possible titles of power being summed up in one word. Certain passages in the poets become intelligible only in the light of this idea: such as the well-known phrase in the chorus of the *Agamemnon* of Æschylus:187.1 "Zeus, whosoever the god is, if this name of Zeus is dear to him, by this name I now appeal to him." The thought and the words of the Vedic poet are often the same as the Greek: Agni is πολυώνυμος: "Agni, many are the names of thee the Immortal one"; and again, "The father adoring gives many names to thee, oh Agni, if thou shouldest take pleasure therein."187.2

But it is in Egypt, the land of magic, where the idea of the potency of the divine name assumes dimensions that are truly gigantic. In an early metaphysical theory of the origin of things, which in its harmonious self-contradiction reaches quite to the level of Hegelian philosophy, the universe is said to have come into being, and the first god himself effects his own creation by the utterance of his own portentous name:188.1 in the beginning was the name. It is said of the great god Ra that "his names are manifold and unknown, even the gods know them not." Naturally, therefore, the goddess Isis was desirous of knowing his real name, and having discovered it by a ruse, she became mistress over him and all gods.188.2 In certain Egyptian papyri containing Abraxas prayers, we find the prayer sometimes coupled with the reminder that the petitioner knows the divine mystic name;188.3 thus equipped, the prayer is more than a mere humble entreaty.

Was it from Egypt that the early Israelites derived the same mystic illusion concerning the divine name, which to some of the scholars of the last generation appeared to be a faith peculiar to the chosen people? At least we are now enabled, by the recent exposition of the facts, to understand the inner force of such prayers as the Psalmist's "Save me, oh God, by thy name and judge me by thy strength":189.1 of Jahvé's warning to his people in the Exodus to obey the angel whom he sends them, "Obey his voice… for my Name is in him:"189.2 of the oath taken by those initiated into the Essenian sect not to reveal the names of the angels:189.3 of expressions in the New Testament concerning the casting out of devils and the healing of the sick in the name of Jesus: finally, of the significant baptismal phrase, "to baptize into the name of Christ,"189.4 which reveals the name as a religious potency into which as into a spiritual atmosphere the adult catechumen or the initiated infant is brought. And these facts of old-world religion and religious logic cast a new light on the name-formulæ which close most of the prayers of the Christian Church, and which are words of power to speed the prayer home; and though the modern consciousness may often be unaware of this mystic function of theirs, we may believe that it was more clearly recognised in the early days of Christianity, for in the apocryphal acts of St John we find a long list of mystical names and titles attached to Christ giving to the prayer much of the tone of an enchantment.190.1

Connected as it seems with this superstition about names is the belief that, in order to gain complete power over a human or divine personality, it is necessary to know their origin and to express what one knows about them in the charm: thus in the Kalevala the young magician is taught the origin of things in order that he may know the proper enchantment against them, and a long account of the origin of iron, regarded as a demoniac substance, occurs in the word-magic used to cure the wound it inflicted. Hence we may account for the descriptive or, so to speak, biographical element in charms that are on the borderland of prayer. The exorciser of evil dreams in the Atharva-Veda prays or sings thus: "We know, oh sleep, thy birth; thou art the son of the divine women-folk, the instrument of Death. Thou art the ender, thou art Death. Thus do we know thee, oh sleep: do thou, oh sleep, protect us from evil dreams."191.1 And in the worship of Agni the belief is expressed that "the prayers fill thee with power and strengthen thee," and this is at once followed by an account of his nature and origin.191.2 Is it then too far-fetched to trace the survival of this old-world thought, rooted as it is in the magic of the word and the statement, in the prominence given to the dogmatic biographical statement in our own liturgy? We regard it as a confession of faith: it may also be regarded as an expression of the worshipper's knowledge of the divine personality, whereby he raises himself into communion with it and thus gains power for his prayer.192.1

Considering now in a more general survey the liturgies of the nations that have attained culture, we might begin with our own fathers. But so little that touches the inner life of their pre-Christian religion has been preserved, that probably not much material for our present purpose is to be discovered from the records. We know that they were given to the employment of the rune or the spell, the rival or the parent of prayer; and one of these, used by Odin to heal the sprained foot of Baldur's foal, is perhaps the only surviving fragment of Indo-Germanic poetry.193.1 Odin sings, "Bone to bone, blood to blood, limb to limb, as though they were glued together"; in a later Norwegian, and also in a Scottish version, it is Christ who heals the foal with the same magic words, strengthened however by the formula, "Heal in the Holy Ghost's name." And this useful medicine-charm was not forgotten by the Aryan Indians, for we find the words in the Atharva-Veda, "Fit together, hair with hair, fit together, skin with skin: thy blood, thy bone shall grow."193.2 Neither god nor ghost was needed to help out the force of such incantations. But probably some time before Christianity prayer had come to prevail over spell in the Teutonic North, for there are traces there of a certain antagonism growing between magic and religion, which led to the condemnation of certain forms of magic.194.1

An interesting question arises about a prayer-charm used by the early English against sterility of the fields: "Hail be thou, Earth, Mother of Men, wax fertile in the embrace of God, fulfilled with fruit for the use of man."194.2 This poetic utterance implies a veritable ἱερὸς γάμος, or holy marriage of earth and heaven in the Greek sense; and reminds us vividly of the spell-formula, used in the Eleusinian Mysteries and descending from the period when the purpose of these was mainly agricultural, Ὗέ Κύε, "Rain and Conceive," which was uttered by the mystes, who folded his arms and glanced up to the sky at the first word and down to the earth at the second: a spell-prayer for fertility and human increase. It is probably then correct to call this phrase of our ancestors, which is the only surviving fragment, so far as I am aware, of their pre-Christian liturgy, a spell-prayer that was efficacious by way of suggestion rather than of entreaty.

Of the same ambiguous character was the old Roman chant of the priests of Mars, "Enos Lases juvate," "Help us, O spirits of our ancestors," repeated with the iteration common in enchantments and accompanied with dancing and with the utterance of the word "triumpe." From the higher point of view the Roman prayers that have come down to us are barren and dull; the well-known liturgical archive containing Rome's address to Jupiter in the critical days of the Hannibalic war is a wary and cleverly drawn legal document, intended to bind the god as well as the State.195.1 In fact the spiritual side of the old Roman character has left no trace of itself in any ritual or liturgy of which we have record. The prayer of Cato's that has been preserved is merely materialistic.196.1

We expect much more from Greece, and in some measure we are not disappointed. Spell-ritual was no doubt always much in vogue, especially for the purposes of agriculture and purification: we hear of certain "magicians" or μάγοι of Cleonae who averted hailstorms with incantations and the shedding of their own blood.196.2 And a solemn part of the State liturgy in Greece was a commination service, which pronounced a curse on certain offences against the State. The religious curse is an interesting phenomenon of which it is not easy to give briefly a full and exact anthropological account; it is taken up by the higher religions, but it by no means originated in them, belonging to the sphere of spell rather than of prayer, and working out its effect by means of magic suggestion. Even the Jewish service, which we still use on Ash Wednesday, employs curse-formulæ in which there is no immediate reference to God, and they may have been regarded originally as having an independent efficacy. This was certainly the case in Greece, for the curse was itself personified as an independent, personal power; and the Erinyes themselves, in some degree the personal embodiments of the curse, work their effect on the victim by singing a spell-song, according to Æschylus, which binds his soul and withers him away.197.1 And the many private "devotiones" or "diræ" that have come down to us from Greek antiquity, written usually on leaden tablets and consecrating the enemy to the powers of the lower world, employ indeed an appeal to these powers that may be interpreted as prayer, but their essential quality is magical, and they certainly were supposed to operate as spells against the individual, while even the divinities to whom they are addressed appear to be constrained rather than entreated. In one interesting example of the first century A.D., found in Ægina,198.1 of Hellenic-Christian or possibly Judaic origin, the curse takes on the form of a prayer for righteous vengeance—"I call on the Highest God, the Lord of all spirits and of all flesh, before whom every soul this day is humbled with supplication, against those who have treacherously slain or poisoned the unfortunate Heracleia." In the Greek legal procedure a curse was sometimes uttered against oneself if one forswore oneself or if one was guilty of the charge; and here as in similar cases in Christian jurisprudence the curse is an invocation of the high god who will punish perjury; but we find it similarly employed in the animistic stage of religion, by the African for instance, who takes an oath by his fetich,198.2 "May this fetich slay me if I do not fulfil the contract"; and in such cases we must regard the curse as a spell working by suggestion against oneself rather than as a prayer.

Before considering Greek prayer proper, we may note as a last example of an ambiguous formula, standing midway as it seems between spell and prayer, the striking liturgical utterance of the old Dodonæan ritual, employed for an agricultural service: the priestesses chanted the refrain in two hexameters, the old metre of religion, "God was, God is, God will be, oh Great God; the earth brings forth fruits, therefore call on mother earth."199.1 The resemblance of this to the early English formula quoted above is striking enough. The first line belongs to an elevated religion and seems far removed from the region of magic; but equally spiritual formulæ concerning the nature and the attributes of God were used in the Zarathustrian and Babylonian liturgies for magical purposes, just as texts from the Bible and Koran have been. And the second line employs the same method as the Navajo Shaman employed, for it states that the divinity is doing that very thing which it is the object of the liturgy to bring about. The appeal to mother earth which is enjoined may have been merely the invocation of her name, a spell at least as much as a prayer. The same may be said of the other popular refrains chanted by the husbandmen of ancient Greece to obtain good crops or fair weather—"Give us big sheaves, sheaves," to Demeter,200.1 or "Come forth, dear sun," to the sun-god.200.2

The public prayers of Greece, those actually used in the temple-service and the official liturgies, have not been preserved, and in this respect the Greek record is very barren compared with the Babylonian, Vedic, or Iranian. But though the actual formulæ are lost, we can gather some impression from the inscriptions and other literary sources as to the objects of prayer. The Athenian state prayed, "For the health and safety of the people of the Athenians, their wives and children and all in the country,"201.1 and the formula might include a prayer for the prosperity of their allies, such as Milesians or Platæans. But we have no indications that the blessings prayed for included others besides the material ones. The Lacedæmonians are commended by Socrates201.2 for refraining from specifying any particular want, either in their private or public prayers, but contenting themselves with praying that the gods should grant them τὰ καλὰ ἐπὶ τοῖς ἀγαθοῖς: the phrase has something of a genuine ring, and is probably derived from a real liturgy, but it is not absolutely precise; it seems, however, to comprise spiritual blessings as well as material, and in this respect to be unique among the public prayers in Greece, if we dare judge them by the scanty record. Probably the formulæ were very old and the range of aspiration usually narrow; and the idea that moral advance could be attained by prayer is perhaps hardly likely to have been reflected in them; yet we must take note of the plaintive question put by the Corcyræan state, weary of civic strife and massacre, to the Dodonæan oracle, asking, "To what god or what hero shall we pray in order to obtain concord, and to govern our city fairly and well?"202.1 and we find an educational official of Cos, in the second century B.C., praying "for the health and the virtuous behaviour of the boys."202.2

We are better informed concerning the style of private prayer in Greece, as also concerning the theory of prayer that gradually commended itself to the highest intelligences. The average private man was certainly capable of praying for blessings other than material. We have the prayer of a potter of Metapontum, of the sixth century B.C., praying to the god that he might "have a good report among men."203.1 Among the prayers contained in the literature of the fifth century, our interest is arrested by such utterances as Pindar's, "May I walk, oh God, in the guileless paths of life, and leave behind me a fair name for my children";203.2 and again, "Oh God that bringest all things to pass, grant me the spirit of reverence for noble things";203.3 and by this of Euripides, "May the spirit of chastity abide with me, the fairest gift of God."203.4 To this age may belong the poetical fragment of a banquet song—for the Greeks could pray genially and seriously in the midst of social intercourse—which must have once had much vogue: "Oh Pallas, born of waters, Queen Athena, mayest thou and thy father keep this city and its citizens in prosperity, free from sorrow, civic discord, and untimely deaths."203.5 The prayers of Xenophon and Plutarch may be taken as typical of the average ethical feeling of their respective periods: the former petitions for "health, bodily strength, good feeling among friends, safety in war, and wealth";204.1 the latter for "wealth, concord, righteousness in word and deed."204.2

Meantime the philosophers from Socrates onwards were insisting on the more spiritual view of prayer, preaching that, in the first place, there was no need to particularise one's needs in one's petitions to God, for there was danger lest one should pray for what is injurious; in the second place, that prayer should look only to the spiritual, not the material life. And we owe to this theory some striking utterances that must rank high in the literature of ethical religion: such as the prayer of Socrates, δοίητέ μοι καλῷ γενέσθαι τἄνδοθεν, "Grant me to become noble of heart"204.3 ; of

Apollonius of Tyana, ὦ θεοὶ δοίητέ μοι τὰ ὀφειλόμενα, "Oh gods, grant me that which I deserve"204.4 ; the longer poetic formula quoted by Plato, "King Zeus, grant us the good whether we pray for it or not, but evil keep from us though we pray for it"205.1 : and with these we may compare the dictum of Epictetus205.2 : "In praying to the divine powers ask for divine things, things free from fleshly or earthly circumstance." Other expressions of the Stoic sect are equally striking for the spirit of fervent acquiescence and resignation that inspires them. Here is the prayer of Epictetus: "Do with me what thou wilt: my will is thy will: I appeal not against thy judgments"205.3 ; and a poetic version of this has come down to us from earlier stoicism—"Lead me, O God, and I will follow, willingly if I am wise, but if not willingly I still must follow." A prayer recorded in the apocryphal Acts of St Thomas205.4 seems almost an echo of these: "I go whither Thou wilt, oh Jesus: Thy will be done."

When the best thought of the age had reached to such a point of spiritual abstraction, it was natural that the same question should arise as arose among the more philosophic adherents of early Christianity, whether special prayers were justifiable at all. It seems that at some period the Pythagorean school were inclined to forbid prayer altogether,206.1 for the reason that God knew better how to give than man knew how to ask; but the later Neo-Platonism discovered an ideal *raison-d'être* for the practice, on the ground that it raised the mind to direct communion and converse with God; and this view is developed at great length by Proclus.206.2

This sketch of the Greek phenomena that belong to our subject may close with an example of that perfervid mysticism that marks the liturgies of latest paganism: the following is the close of a long address to Asclepios—an Hellenic deity attracted here into the Egyptian circle—found in the treatise called *Asclepios*, attributed to Apuleius:207.1 "We rejoice in thy divine salvation, because thou hast shown thyself wholly to us: we rejoice that thou hast deigned to consecrate us to eternity, while we are still in these mortal bodies. We have known thee, oh true life of the life of man.... Adoring thy goodness, we make this our only prayer... that thou wouldst be willing to keep us all our lives in the love of thy knowledge." Portions at least of this prayer, which was the prelude to a communion supper, would not surprise us if we found it in a Christian liturgy.207.2

It will be convenient next to glance at the records of the other great branches of the ancient Aryan world, the Vedic Indians and the Iranians. One does not read long in the sacred books of India without attaining the conviction that the highest religion of the Vedas was deeply penetrated with sacerdotal magic; which was so far from losing its hold in the later period that it imprisoned the religious thought, and the later Brahmanism was capable of the belief that without the spell of the sacrifice the sun could not run his course in heaven. And the recital of spells forms a great part of the Vedic ritual. Thus the hymns say of the fire-god Agni, "The thoughtful men find Agni when they have recited the spells"; and the gods themselves, like the Norse divinities, work by spells: "Agni upholds the sky by his efficacious spells."208.1 Yet the early record gives us also copious illustration of real prayer, and occasionally of a very exalted tone. It is true, as we should expect, that material and temporal advantages are by far the predominant objects of the petition: the head of the household prays for wealth, offspring, victory in battle or the races; with rare exceptions, the prayers are personal and private rather than political, and are thus in marked contrast to the Hellenic; yet we have a few that are evidently proffered for the community,209.1 and at times the deity is petitioned to grant an abundant supply of valiant men. But even in the few prayers that reflect the political life of the State, the individualistic spirit is apt to appear. We have a curious example of a petition to Indra to make a man powerful in the political assembly: "In this entire gathering render, O Indra, me successful," and this is combined with a naïve spell whereby the politician endeavours to mesmerise the whole meeting: he names the assembly—as our Speaker might name a recalcitrant member—"We know thy name, oh assembly…. Of them that are sitting together I take to myself the power and the understanding": and again, "With my mind do I seize your minds."210.1 But even when the prayer is personal and materialistic a real fervour and a genial poetic freshness is often to be found. Here is a beautiful prelude to a prayer for long life proffered to the ancient heaven-god: "Many dawns have not yet dawned: grant me to live in them, O Varuna." And often the worshipper rises above mere material aspirations, as in such appeals to Agni as the following: "May we be well-doers before the gods."210.2 "Give us not up, oh Agni, to want of thought."210.3 "Mayest thou bestow splendour, renown, and (wise) mind upon such mortals as satisfy thee with refreshment, oh Agni."210.4 "Drive far from us senselessness and anguish: drive far all ill-will from whom thou attendest."210.5 At times also the hymns reveal a deep consciousness of sin and a desire for divine forgiveness. "Through want of strength, thou strong and bright god, have I gone astray. Have mercy, Almighty, have mercy!"211.1 "Agni, drive away from us sin, which leads us astray."211.2 "By the earth's greatness, oh Agni, forgive us even committed sin, that we may be great."211.3 "Whatever sin we have committed against thee in thoughtlessness, men as we are, make thou us sinless before Aditi."211.4 Yet we may suspect that the term sin is not always used in these prayers in its modern ethical sense, not for instance in the prayer, "From the sins which knowingly or unknowingly we have committed, do ye, all gods, of one accord release us";211.5 and the primitive concept on which the old magic of sin-transference was based survives in such passages as the following: "Pass far away, oh sin of the mind: why dost thou utter things not to be uttered? Pass away, I love thee not: to the trees and the forests go on!"212.1 "Enter into the rays, into smoke, oh sin; go into the vapours, and into the fog."212.2 The context discloses only an indirect appeal to a personal deity, though the term sin in the former passage is clearly applied to what we should call moral offences.

In the Vedic ritual, then, we find a pure and spiritual form of prayer; yet a certain spell-power may attach even to the highest types, for we find not infrequently the conception that not only the power of the worshipper but the power of the deity also is nourished and strengthened by prayer;212.3 and the prayer itself is usually accompanied by a potent act. With this aspect of Vedic prayers we may associate the fact that Agni, the fire-god, appears as the chief divinity to whom they are addressed; for his ritual is purificatory, and the prayers are thus based on a liturgy of purification which stimulates the mental or spiritual force of the worshipper.

We may now turn to another great Aryan stock, the Iranian, whose earlier religion culminated in the Zarathustrian system. The relation of spell to prayer is, on the whole, the same in the Zend-Avesta as we find it in the Vedic hymns, a real spell can accompany a real prayer, and the text of the prayer itself becomes a most potent charm. The "sacerdotal" physician, who, as we have seen, occupied a higher rank in the Zarathustrian estimate than the scientific practitioner, offers first a genuine prayer to Ahura-Mazda for spiritual strength to deal with the disease—"Give us, Ahura, that powerful sovereignty by the strength of which we may smite down the drug (the demon)." Fraught with this mesmeric power he then directs his spell against the sickness-demon: "To thee, oh Sickness, I say—Avaunt! To thee, oh Death, I say—Avaunt!"214.1 And in the ritual of purification, which closely resembles the system of therapeutics, the formulæ of prayers of the most exalted type in the sacred books are used, not as prayers, but as cathartic spells.214.2 It is not hard to discern the steps that lead from this grade of thought to the highest at which the religious speculation of the Zarathustrian arrived. The uttered Word of God is given a supernatural cosmic force; and the prophet pronounces that this utterance of the "Holy Word is of such a nature that if all the corporeal and living world should learn it, and learning hold fast to it, they should be redeemed from their mortality."214.3 And we can understand why a large part of the Zarathustrian liturgy should be devoted to the recital of formulæ which are statements of the Mazdean faith. Before rising in the morning and retiring at night, the pious Persian was recommended to say, "All good thoughts, all good words, all good deeds I do willingly: all evil thoughts, all evil words, all evil deeds

I do unwillingly."215.1 It is interesting to compare with our own creed the following Mazdean confession: "I confess myself a Mazdayasnian of Zarathustra's order: I celebrate my praises for good thoughts, good words, and good deeds.... With chanting praises I present all good thoughts, good words, and good deeds, and with rejection I repudiate all evil thoughts and words and deeds. Here I give to you, oh ye Bountiful Immortals, sacrifice and homage with the mind,215.2 with words, deeds, and my entire person, yea, I offer to you the flesh of my very body."215.3 The formulæ of confession, as well as other parts of this liturgy, are penetrated with the idea of a moral-theological dualism to which our Christian theology has been indirectly deeply indebted. The Mazdean proclaims his detestation of the Daevas, and of Angra-Mainyu, the evil god. "Taught by Ahura, I drive away Angra-Mainyu from this house, this borough"; such words are "victorious, most healing,"216.1 and could be used as the recitation of our creed and paternoster have been used, as veritable spells against the evil power or demon. But in comparing the spell-prayers of the Persian with the Vedic, we are struck with the superiority of the former liturgy in one respect, that here the spell is only brought to bear on the demon, not on the highest god; the prayer increases the spiritual force of the worshipper but does not constrain Ahura.

And the Iranian prayers appear to rise above the Vedic in the enthusiasm of the idea of righteousness that pervades them, and in the conviction that the believer can aid Ahura-Mazda in the continual struggle against the power of evil and in helping towards the final establishment of the righteous kingdom. He prays that, "Through the good thought and the holiness of him who offers thee the due meed of praise thou mayest, oh Lord, make the world of Resurrection appear at thy will, under thy sovereign rule."217.1 "May we be such as those who bring on this great Renovation."217.2 "May we help to bring on the good government of Ahura, which is the best for us at every present hour."217.3 "Be righteousness life-strong and clothed with body. In that realm which shines with splendour as the sun, let piety be present, and may she, through the indwelling of thy good mind, give us blessings in reward for deeds."217.4 In fact the greater number of the prayers are strikingly spiritual, and for spiritual, not material blessings. The prophet asks Ahura, "How man may become most like unto thee?"217.5 and prays for "aids of grace, beseeching what in accordance with thy wished-for aim is best."218.1 And the prayer is sometimes directed to abstract moral powers, emanations of Ahura: "If the Mazda-Ahura and Righteousness and Pious Concord be invokable, I implore through the good mind a kingdom for myself, through whose increase we may conquer the Lie." The kingdom is here the "Desirable Kingdom of Righteousness."218.2 Certainly the

Mazdean kingdom was not of this world, and the Zarathustrian religion is one of the least materialistic that the world has known; its chief moral weakness being, as we have seen, its bondage to ritualistic purity. We may note in conclusion, as showing the continuity of the national spirit, the pronouncement of a Persian Christian, Bishop Aphrahat of East Syria, that the only valid object of prayer was purity of heart.218.3

Many of the phenomena that we have been noting among the Aryan races confront us again when we turn to the Chaldæan-Babylonian liturgies. Here also there appears no real antagonism between spell and prayer, magic and religion.219.1 Spell-formulæ are used and accompanied with a ritual of purification to drive out the evil spirits of sickness; and the highest hymns containing real prayers can be employed as texts for magic purposes; even the gods themselves work by magic, and Marduk himself is invoked as the arch-magician.219.2 And the idea that the prayer could in some sense exercise compulsion on the god appears in an anecdote told by Porphyry about a Chaldæan who was an expert in "purifications of the soul: but found his efforts thwarted because another man who was powerful in the same art had, by means of mystic prayers, bound over the powers he had invoked not to grant his demands."219.3 Yet by the side of all this we find often an exalted type of prayer, with spiritual and fervent expressions of homage; and the religious law that "prayer absolves from sin" is given as part of Marduk's revelation to man.220.1 A large number of the records contain the liturgies used by the kings, and while victory, health, and long life, the permanence of the dynasty are the more usual objects of the petition, the deeper ethical tone is often heard. The following are a few examples of the higher aspirations of the Babylonian religion. The founder of the new Babylonian kingdom has recorded his convictions for the guidance of his successor: "Marduk sees through the lips, sees the heart: he who keeps true to Bel and the son of Bel will last for ever."220.2 One of the greatest prayers in this or any other liturgical collection is that which Nebukadnezar made to Marduk on his accession:220.3 "Oh Eternal Ruler, Lord of All… lead the King by the right way… I am… the work of thy hand: after thy great mercy which thou showest to all, oh Lord, grant that thy high majesty may show compassion upon me: set in my heart the fear of thy Godhead: grant me what thou deemest best: for thou it is that hast created my life." This is scarcely the Nebukadnezar whom we once thought we knew. There is also a pathetic interest attaching to the prayer of Nabonnedos to the god Schamasch for his son Belsazar:221.1 "Prolong the days of Belsazar, my first-born son—may he commit no sin." The king Nabonnedos prays also to Marduk: "May I rule as king according to thy wish… let me not in my pride lose knowledge of thee, for it is thou that hast chosen me out."221.2

The following phrases in a prayer to Marduk of an unknown ruler are still more striking: "Oh Marduk, great Lord... let me behold thy Godhead, let me attain my heart's desire: set righteousness on my lips and grace in my heart."221.3 Among the attributes of the gods there is a fervent recognition of their mercy and compassionateness: Marduk is "the god full of mercy, who loves to quicken that which is dead";222.1 and Ischtar, the goddess, is invoked as "the helper of the oppressed, oh thou endowed with majesty; thou who raisest the fallen and exaltest the trodden under foot."222.2 And the same idea reappears in a hymn to another goddess of like character with Ischtar, in which we catch the tones of a high religious poetry of homage:222.3 "Oh strong and majestic, highest of the goddesses, radiant star... strongest of the goddesses whose robe is the light: thou who dost course through heaven and engirdle the earth... dealing punishment and pleading for men, rewarding the just, leading the wanderer, overthrowing the enemy who feareth not thy Godhead, protecting the captive, taking the weak by the hand—be gracious unto thy servant, who calls upon thy name with grace."

This brief illustrative selection may close with the quotation of a prayer or hymn of praise to Marduk, perhaps the most remarkable among those that have as yet been translated:223.1 "The Lord, peerless in might, the King of grace, the Ruler of the lands, that bringeth peace in heaven, that through his glance overthroweth the mighty. Lord, thy seat is Babylon, thy crown Borsippa. Thy thought, oh Lord, passeth over the wide heavens, and with thine eyes thou beholdest the affliction of men, through the anger of thy countenance thou spreadest lamentation, and thou takest him captive who regardeth thee not and setteth himself up against thee. Through thy gracious countenance thou showest men favour, thou lettest them see the light and they proclaim thy Righteousness. Oh Lord of the lands, Light of Izizi, thou who proclaimest grace, who is it whose mouth doth not tell of thy Righteousness, who doth not praise thy majesty, and glorify thy lordship?... Look down upon the hands raised in prayer to thee. Grant favour to thy city Babylon... and turn thy countenance upon thy house, and give help to the sons of Babylon and all thy people."

With all their spells and their magic, the higher minds of the Babylonians knew how to pray, and the fervent and exalted tones of such liturgies remind us of the religious poetry of Israel. And it is interesting to note that among the few deities of Babylon whose ideal reached to such a point of ethical development, the moon-god Sin appears, who gave his name to Sinai, and who has been thought by some to have had some original affinity with the God of Israel.224.1

As regards the liturgies of Egypt, so far as I have been able with very limited opportunities to examine them, the superstition of the spell lay so heavy on the Egyptian mind, that prayer does not seem able to extricate itself from its prepossession. Not only do the deities work by means of spells and the magic of their names, but the worshipper uses the same means to work upon them; and the prayer that accompanies the spell seems usually to savour of self-confidence and command. At least this is the impression one gathers from what is published concerning the Book of the Dead and the ritual practised to secure the happiness of the deceased. By utterance of words of enchantment over pictures, the soul of the dead becomes divine.225.1 The magic word helps to transfer the power of the deity into the fetich, and this with the word written upon it is placed on the body of the dead: for instance, an amulet with the words, "May the blood of Isis... and the word of power of Isis be mighty to protect this mighty one";225.2 a terra-cotta lamp of the Greco-Roman period, carved with the symbol of the frog-headed goddess Heqt, and bearing the words, "I am the Resurrection."226.1 On an object placed under the head of the deceased to maintain the warmth of the body, we find the following words, supposed to be addressed by the spirit to Amen:226.2 "I am a perfect spirit among the companions of Ra, and I have gone in and come forth among the perfect souls... grant thou unto me the things which my body needeth, and heaven for my soul and a hidden place for my mummy." "May the god who himself is hidden and whose face is concealed, who shineth upon the world in his forms of existence and in the underworld, grant that my soul may live for ever."226.3 Here we have the statement of a conviction that gains its assurance from magic, followed by prayer. It seems that the Egyptian prayed to the gods, as if by such prayer he might gain immortality, but that he trusted equally to magical means, to pictures and words of power from the sacred texts, and employed at once the methods of religion and of enchantment.227.1

Looking at the Christian religion, we should find it hard to give a succinct and accurate account of these phenomena in the various stages of its history. We may be able to set forth the theories and ritual-practices of the various churches and compare them with what we find elsewhere; but it is more difficult to analyse accurately the religious psychology, the thought and feeling which accompanies the ritual: the quality of the mental state would depend partly on the ancestral conditions and the strength of the ancestral instincts of the individual. And the teaching of the most spiritual Christian philosophy has not been able to prevent some touches of the old-world magic from contaminating the worship. The theory of the leading thinkers among the early Christian fathers agreed, as we have seen, with the pronouncement of later Greek philosophy. Both for Clemens, who gives us the earliest theory of Christian prayer, without finding, however, a clear logical system, and for Origen, the final justification of prayer was communion with God, τὸ ἀνακραθῆναι τῷ πνεύματι,228.1 ὁμιλία πρὸς τὸν θεὸν ἡ εὐχή.228.2 And Clemens maintains that the true gnostic, he who has the true knowledge of God, "works himself with God in his prayer so as to attain perfection."228.3 The gnostic of Clemens, then, is not purely petitionary in his prayer; by his spontaneous self-projection he contributes something himself to the attainment of the end he prays for; and, as I have ventured to suggest above, we may discern in this theory the meeting-point of the more primitive and the more exalted religious views.

Meantime the actual heretic sect of the gnostics were applying much of the old magic under new names and new texts, and did not even care to discard wholly the old spell-nomenclature.229.1 And even in the orthodox churches, as we have seen, the mystic power and liturgical use of the name has continued, being the inheritance of a different religious world from that with which we are familiar or of which we are conscious. We may also legitimately compare many of the ritual acts which accompany prayer, for instance in the earlier and later Roman Church, with the suggestive or mimetic religious actions of less advanced cults. One of the most interesting examples that may be quoted is the description of the blessing of the baptismal water on the eve of the Epiphany, a custom prevalent in the earlier Church of Rome:229.2 the priest, while praying to God to sanctify the water, dipped a crucifix thrice into it, recalling in his prayer the miracle described in Exodus, the sweetening of the bitter water with wood; then followed antiphonal singing describing Christ's baptism in Jordan, which sanctified the water. We appear to have here a combination of the great typical forms of the immemorial religious energy, prayer pure and simple, the potent use of the spiritually charged object, the fetich (in this case the crucifix), and an intoned or chanted narrative which has the spell-value of suggestion.230.1

What maintained the use of the spell-prayer in full vigour throughout the earlier and medieval epochs of Christendom, even in the orthodox ritual, was chiefly the practice of exorcism and the belief in demons and demoniac possession; and the legal institution of the ordeal contributed also to its maintenance. As modern society has abandoned such institutions, and the modern mind is no longer possessed with demonology, so in the modern worship prayer has become more and more purified from the associations of the spell; the traces that remain of the latter are faint and usually unintelligible to the modern worshipper. And on the other side there is a progressive tendency beginning to be felt, making for a reform of our liturgy in respect of the objects for which prayer should be proffered. But in this respect, as the comparison has shown, we cannot be said to have advanced as yet beyond many of the old-world religions.

The special subjects of these last two lectures, the history of purification and prayer, have only been presented in an inadequate sketch. The full and exhaustive treatment of either would serviceably fill a gap in the library of comparative religion. But they have served my present purpose, if they have been able to illustrate and to some extent test the value of the comparative study of the various theologies of mankind.

INDEX

Prayer (*vide* Spell) definition of, distinction between prayer and spell, antagonism between them, objects of prayer, progress from material to spiritual, prayer a form of communion with the deity, Christian theory of prayer, survival of spell in Christian liturgy, Egyptian prayer, dominated by spell, English, earliest example of spellprayer, Eleusinian spellprayer, Hellenic prayer, Hellenic spells, spell prayer, theory of prayer in Hellenic philosophy, Iranian liturgical magic, prayers and spells in Zarathustrian ritual, Latin prayer, Roman spell-prayer, Peruvian prayer,3 savage examples of real prayer, Umbrian prayer, Vedic spell-formulæ combined with prayer,

Purification primitive ideas concerning pure and impure substances, analysis of primitive sensation of impurity, purification after battle, after funerals, logical development of idea of purity, psychological effect of impure contact, purity connected with belief in spirits, dualism of good and evil spirits, with belief in gods, earliest concept non-moral, evolution of idea of "pure heart," cathartic sacrifice, opposition between spiritual and ritualistic purity, Iranian ideas, Jewish, Hellenic, influence on Hellenic law, influence of idea of purity on religious institutions,

ENDNOTES

LECTURES I AND II NOTES

3.1 Garcilasso de la Vega, *Royal Commentary of the Incas* (Hakluyt Society): Sahagun—transl. Jourdanet et Siméon.

3.2 Jacob Laskowski, *vide* Usener, *Götternamen*, p. 82, etc.

6.1 *Golden Bough*, 2nd ed., vol. iii. p. 186.

13.1 For instance, an ancestor may for certain reasons be worshipped in the form of a snake, and yet this need not imply a snake-tribe or any tribal worship of snakes in general.

26.1 *Vide infra*, pp. 192, 193.

26.2 *E.g. De Civ. Dei.*, bk. 2, ch. 6: deos paganorum nunquam bene vivendi sanxisse doctrinam.

27.1 Plutarch, *Parallela*, 35. *Vide* my *Cults of Greek States*, vol. i. p. 93.

28.1 Servius, *Æn.* iii. 121.

28.2 *Ibid.*, ii. 801.

29.1 *Sacred Books of the East*, vol. iv. (ed. Mills), p. 211.

29.2 *Vide* account of these in *Revue des Études grecques*, xiii. (1900), p. 233, and *Annuaire de l'Association pour l'encouragement des Études grecques*, 1871, p. 92.

31.1 *Protrept.*, 12, § 120 (p. 92 P).

33.1 I have noticed the evidence of this in my forthcoming third volume of the *Cults of the Greek States*.

34.1 *C.I.G.*, 4697.

34.2 *Haeres.* 51, 22; Dindorf, vol. ii. p. 483, 12-29: *vide* Philologus, 16, p. 354. I find that the view I have taken of this important text agrees on the whole with that of Usener in his *Untersuchungen*, p. 27.

37.1 That Aion was a real figure of Mithraic religion has been finally proved by the *Mithras-Liturgie*, published by Dieterich, p. 4, l. 21.

37.2 Usener quotes a few examples from the liturgy of the Greek Church and one or two from patristic literature, *Religionsgesch. Untersuchungen*, 1, p. 28, n. 5: some of these are poetical.

38.1 *Vide* Artemis R. 37, in my *Cults of the Greek States*, vol. ii. p. 567.

38.2 Paus. 4, 33, 4: inscription in Dittenberger, *Sylloge*(2), 653.

38.3 Vide *Report of American School at Athens*, vol. i., inscr. No. xxvi.

39.1 *Vide* chapter on Cybele in the forthcoming third volume of my *Cults of the Greek States*.

42.1 *Anth. Pal.* xi. 269, "I am Heracles, the triumphant son of Zeus; I am not Luke, but they compel me."

42.2 *Ephemeris Archaiologiké*, 1900, πίν. 5.

43.1 Theocritus, *Id.* 7, 106.

43.2 *Cults of Greek States*, vol. ii. p. 735: R. 25b.

44.1 *Cf.* the method of Greco-Egyptian magic of strangling birds before the idol of Eros, in order that their breath may animate it, mentioned in an Abraxas papyrus, *Class. Rev.* 1896, p. 409.

45.1 *Vide* Schrader, *Real-Lexikon, s.v.* Eid.

45.2 *Ad Nat.* i. 12.

47.1 The *Tatu*, *Tat*, or *Ded* pillar erected in the ritual of Osiris, perhaps as a symbol of the resurrection of the god, had the form of a cross: *vide* Frazer, *Golden Bough* (2), ii. p. 141.

48.1 Vide *Palace of Knossos*: Provisional Report for year 1903, p. 92: the writer quotes Babylonian and Assyrian examples.

49.1 Epist. 395: the doctrines of the Orphic sects from the fourth century B.C. onwards also emphasised the kinship of man with God, as the well-known Orphic tablets, found in South Italy and Crete, reveal (*Hell. Journ.* 3, p. 112: Miss J. Harrison, *Prolegomena to the Study of Greek Religion*: Appendix by Prof. Murray, p. 660). In the pseudo-Platonic *Axiochus*, p. 371 D, the sick man is assured of salvation as being "of the family of God" γεννήτης τῶν θεῶν.

50.1 *E.g.* a priest of Megalopolis, a hierophantes of the Great Goddesses, is spoken of as descended from "those who first established the mystic worship of the Great Goddesses among the Arcadians," *Eph. Archaiol.* 1896, p. 122: the priests of Poseidon at Halikarnassos traced their descent from those who brought his cult from Troezen at the foundation of the city, *C.I.G.* 2655.

50.2 At Cos, *vide* Paton and Hicks, *Inscriptions of Cos*, No. 103 (Roman Imperial period).

51.1 *E.g.* the priest of Cybele at Pessinus, and the priest of Ma in the two Comanas.

52.1 *Vide* Golther, *Handbuch der germanischen Mythologie*, p. 612, 617.

53.1 *Vide* my paper in the *Archiv für Religionswissenschaft*, 1904, on "The Position of Women in Ancient Religion."

54.1 *Vide infra*, p. 72.

54.2 See King, *Babylonian Religion*, p. 211.

55.1 *Vide* chapter on "Apollo Cult" in my forthcoming fourth volume of *Cults*.

55.2 Plutarch, *Apophtheg. Lacon.* p. 229 D: Lysander is told by the priest that before initiation he must confess his worst sin: he asks if this was the gods' command or the priests', and on hearing that it was the gods who enjoined it, he replied, "Then do you stand aside and I will tell the gods if they ask me."

55.3 *Opp. Ep.* 96.

55.4 *Vide* Herzog, *Real-Encyclopädie, s.v. Beichte.*

56.1 Jourdanet et Siméon, p. 24.

57.1 Heszch, *s.v.* Ἀμφιδρόμια.

57.2 *Vide* Golther, *op. cit.* p. 555.

57.3 *Polit.* p. 1336 B.

57.4 In the Attis Mysteries the reborn and initiated were fed on milk— Sallustius, *De Diis et Mundo*, 4: for a careful treatment of the whole question, *vide* Dieterich, *Eine Mithras-Liturgie*, pp. 157-178: for various savage parallels showing the prevalence in primitive societies of the idea of death and rebirth at initiation, *vide* Frazer, *Golden Bough*, vol. iii. pp. 424-446.

58.1 *Vide* Herzog, *Real-Encycl.*, xii. p. 319.

58.2 *Vide* Trede, *Das Heidenthum in der römischen Kirche*, vol. i. p. 280, "Neue und alte Fest-Lust."

60.1 *Vide* Frazer's *Golden Bough, passim*, especially vol. ii. pp. 115-168 (death and resurrection in rites of Adonis, Attis, Osiris, Dionysos), and vol. iii. pp. 138-200: *cf.* articles by Bernard Cook in *Classical Review*, 1903, 1904, on "Zeus Jupiter and the Oak": we must distinguish between the simulated death of the divine effigy, and the simulated or real death of the human representative of divinity. In Hellenic religion we can trace the idea in the worship of Pan, in the legends and ritual of Artemis-Iphigenia and Aphrodite, vide *Cults of the Greek States*, vol. ii. pp. 440-442, 650-652, and in the Cretan worship of Zeus, vol. i. pp. 36-38: but it had lost its vitality in the purely Hellenic cults of the classical period, and was only real and energetic in the legends and ritual of Adonis and Dionysos.

61.1 *Vide* Dio Chrys., vol. ii. p. 16 (Dindorf), and K. O. Müller's *Sardon und Sardanapal* (*Kleine Schriften*, vol. ii. p. 100): on a coin published in British Museum Catalogue, "Lycaonia," etc., pl. xxxiii. 2, p. 180, we see the god on his lion standing on what may be his pyre.

62.1 *Vide* especially Hippol., *Ref. Haeres.* 5, p. 118 (Miller): Macrob., *Saturn.* 1, 21, 7: Arnobius, *Adv. Gent.* 5, 7, 16; 7, 49: Julian, *Or.* 5, 168 C.

62.2 *De error.* c. 22.

63.1 For the Greek origin of the Christian apocalyptical literature, *vide* Dieterich, *Beitrage zur Erklärung der neu-entdeckten Petrus Apokalypse*, Leipzig, 1893. The clearest trace of Orphic influence on historic Christianity is the doctrine of purgatory, which was popularised for the later ages by Vergil's VIth *Æneid*: *vide* especially the purgatorial theory in Servius' Commentary, *Æn.* vi. 741.

65.1 *Hibbert Journal*, January 1904.

66.1 Alexis in Stobæus, *Florileg.* (Meineke), vol. iii. p. 83.

67.1 *Vide* Herzog, *Real-Encycl.*, *s.v.* "Montanismus": *cf.* the article there on "Maria" and the chapter in Trede, *op. cit.* vol. ii., "Die grosse Mutter."

68.1 Euseb. *v. Const.*, iii. 43, 2.

69.1 Vide *Cults of the Greek States*, pp. 650-652.

69.2 One of the Babylonian goddesses is addressed in the same hymn as "Mother, wife, and maid," Jastrow, *Relig. Babyl. Assyr.*, p. 459.

70.1 Vide *Cults of the Greek States*, vol. ii., Artemis, R 133: *cf.* Paus. 8, 13, 1.

70.2 I am treating this question in an appendix to the Cybele chapter in vol. iii. of my *Cults*, etc.

71.1 *E.g.* fragment of Naumachius in Stobæus, *op. cit.*, vol. iii. pp. 16-17.

72.1 *Vide* specially Trede, *Das Heidenthum in der römischen Kirche*: Renan, *Les origines du christianisme*, vol. vii. 572-573. The resemblances are particularly striking between the Catholic and the Isiac sacerdotalism.

72.2 Hæres., 79.

72.3 Herod., 4, 33.

73.1 *Cf.* the prayer to Ninlil or Belit (a parallel form to Ischtar) of Asarhaddon, "may the lips of Nin-lil, the Mother of the Great God, utter daily a gracious word before Aschur for the King of Assyria" (Jastrow, *op. cit.* p. 525). Mary was chiefly worshipped in the same way as an intercessor.

73.2 For the identity of Father and Son in the later Mithraic cult-dogma, *vide* Dieterich, *Eine Mithras-Liturgie*, p. 68: for the Trinitarian idea in Mithraism, *vide* Cumont, *Die Mysterien von Mithra (deutsche Ausgabe)*, pp. 96, 145: Mr Cook endeavours to trace it in the old Pelasgian cult of Zeus, *Class. Rev.* 1903, 1904: vide *Hell. Journ.*, 1901, p. 139, for Trinitarian symbolism in Carthaginian worship. (Note a certain mystic sanctity attached to the triad in later Greek philosophy, *e.g.* in Porphyry, Serv., Verg., *Ecl.*, 5, 66: Io. Lydus, *de Mens.*, 2, 19.)

74.1 *Sacred Books of the East*, vol. xxxi. pt. iii. p. 278.

75.1 Vide *Cults of the Greek States*, vol. i. p. 306.

LECTURE III NOTES

91.1 *De Mysteriis*, 5, 23.

97.1 *Sacred Books of the East*, vol. iv., Zend-Avesta, pt. i. pp. 58-59.

99.1 *E.g.* onions, pease-soup, cheese: I-Tsing, *Records of the Buddhist Religion*, p. 138, "onions have a foul smell and are impure": *cf.* list of impure substances in ritual inscription of Rhodes, *C.I.G. Ins. Mar. Æg.* i. No. 789.

99.2 *Sacred Books of the East*, Zend-Avesta, pt. i. p. 105.

101.1 *C.I.A.*, 3, 73.

101.2 The purifying power that ashes possess in certain ritual may be derivative from fire.

103.1 *Op. cit.*, pt. i. p. 120.

104.1 *E.g. op. cit.*, pp. 201, 204.

105.1 *E.g.* Porphyry in Euseb., *Præp. Evang.*, 4, 22.

106.1 Steinmetz, *Die Entwickelung der Strafe*, vol. ii. p. 355.

106.2 *Cf.* "Ye shall be holy, for I am holy," Lev. xi. 44; Deuteron. xxiii. 12.

107.1 Jastrow, *op. cit.*, p. 500.

108.1 *Germania*, c. 40.

108.2 Golther, *op. cit.* p. 570.

108.3 Golther, *op. cit.* p. 607.

112.1 Casalis, *Les Bassoutos*, p. 269: among the Zulus, sin and dirt are spoken of as the same,—"You have dirt, you are dirty" = "You have done wrong," Leslie, *Among the Zulus*, p. 170. (These and other references to the evidence from savage society I owe to the kindness of my friend Mr R. Marett.)

114.1 Andoc., *De Myst.*, 110.

115.1 *Op. cit.*, p. 102.

116.1 The same kind of ceremonious logic inspires the practice of the Damaras, who, when making peace with an alien tribe, go into a river with their foes and throw water into their faces to wash away enmity.—Sir J. E. Alexander, *Expedition and Discoveries*, vol. ii. p. 171.

117.1 Veniaminoff ap. Petroff, *Alaska*, p. 158.

117.2 Molina, *Fables and Rites of the Yncas* (Hakluyt Society), p. 22.

118.1 Lev. xvii.

118.2 2, 39.

119.1 The cathartic process of transference applied to plague as well as actual sin, *e.g.* Aristotle, *Frag.*, 454, transference of disease into a raven.

119.2 Serv., *Æn.* 3, 57.

120.1 In modern India a criminal and his wife sometimes undertake to transfer into their own persons the sins of the Rajah and the Rani: *Anthrop. Journ.*, 1901, p. 302.

120.2 *Vide* chapter on Apollo Ritual, *Cults*, vol. iv.

121.1 *Cf.* Blood-purification in Vedic ritual, Hillebrandt, *Vedische Opfer und Zauber*, p. 179 (evil spirits driven away by a reed dipped in blood of the sacrifice, p. 176): in the Lupercalia at Rome the foreheads of youths were smeared with the blood of the sacrificed goat and dog and then wiped with wool dipped in milk, probably a piacular ceremony; *vide* W. Fowler, *The Roman Festivals*, p. 311.

121.2 *Cf.* Apollon. Rhod., 4, 478, for pig's blood in purification from murder.

122.1 Numbers c. 19.

124.1 Levit. xvi. 2.

125.1 Numbers xxxi. 19.

125.2 Numbers xxxv.

125.3 Numbers xxxv. 25.

126.1 Deuteron. xxi.

127.1 *Sacred Books of the East*, vol. iv. part i. p. 81.

128.1 *Sacred Books of the East*, vol. iv. part i. p. 204.

128.2 *Ib.* p. 88.

128.3 *Ib.* p. 136.

129.1 *Sacred Books of the East*, vol. iv. p. 28.

130.1 *Sacred Books of the East*, vol. iv. p. 56; *cf.* p. 141.

130.2 The virtue of chastity is religious rather than ethical; the courtesan is reprobated because she mingles the seed of believers and unbelievers alike, *ib.* p. 205. Yet the Zarathustrian system escaped the extravagant exaltation of mere virginity that is found in early Christian literature: "the man who has a wife is far above him who lives in continence" (Fargard, iv.-iii. *b*, p. 46).

131.1 *Sacred Books*, vol. iv. p. 216.

131.2 *Ib.* p. 216.

132.1 *Sacred Books*, vol. iv. p. 87.

135.1 Livy, 40, 6, 1-3: the whole host was led between the severed limbs of a dog.

135.2 Herod., 8, 27.

136.1 Plutarch, *Quæst. Græc.*, 24.

136.2 Stobæus, *Florileg.* Meineke, vol. ii. p. 184.

137.1 Mullach, *Frag. Philos.*, Adespota.

137.2 *Anth. Pal.*, 14, 71.

137.3 *Ib.* No. 74.

138.1 Wilamowitz, *Isyllos*, 6; *Anth. Pal.*, Adespota, ccxxxiii. *b*: *cf.* inscription from Astypalaia in Collitz, *Dialect-Inschriften*, No. 3472.

138.2 *C.I.G. Ins. Mar. Æg.* 1, 789.

139.1 In Neæram, § 85.

139.2 Clem. Alex., *Strom.*, 619, Pott.

140.1 I believe that the trial scene on the shield of Achilles, rightly interpreted, implies that the community are beginning to decide whether the avenger shall accept the were-gilt or not.

142.1 *Die Entwickelung der Strafe*, vol. ii. p. 347.

143.1   An example is given by Steinmetz, *op. cit.* ii. p. 336, of the punishment of incest among the *Pasemaher*: the guilty pair were buried alive with a hollow pipe reaching from their mouths to the top of the earth: if they survived seven days of this agony their lives were spared: no explanation is offered, but it is not improbable that the law is inspired by the idea that the earth could absorb their impurity.

144.1   *Sacred Books*, vol. iv. p. 169 (pt. i.).

145.1   Vide *Cults of the Greek States*, vol. i. pp. 66-69: Steinmetz, *op. cit.*, vol. ii. p. 345, discusses a record concerning the Ossetes, who live habitually in the system of the blood-feud, to the effect that a person guilty of parricide was surrounded and burnt in his house by the whole people, and he suggests that this may be the first example among them of a State cognisance of murder.

147.1   Antiphon, *Or.* 6, p. 764: *cf.* Eurip., *Hecuba*, pp. 291-292.

148.1   Demosthenes, *c. Aristocrat.*, pp. 643-644.

148.2   Antiphon, p. 686.

149.3   *Laws*, pp. 854, 865.

149.4   Demosthenes, *c. Aristocrat.*, p. 643.

149.5   Antiphon, p. 709.

150.1   Demosthenes, *op. cit.*, p. 645: *cf.* the account in Pausanias, 5, 27, 10, of the purification by the Eleans at Olympia of the bronze ox which had caused the death of a boy.

151.1   Drako appears to have systematised it, but it may have existed as custom-law before his period.

151.2   Paus., 1, 19, 1; 1, 28, 10: Plut., *vit. Thes.*, 12, 18: Demosth., *c. Aristocrat.*, 74.

152.1   We note the legend that purification was refused to Ixion, and the express statement that no one would purify King Pausanias from his brutal crime against the Olynthian maiden.

152.2   The procedure by ordeal, prevalent in the ancient world and common among contemporary savages, is probably derived from an animistic conception of purity: the primitive theory appears to be that, if the person is innocent, the pure spirit within him makes his body able to resist the trial, and is not dependent upon any idea of a higher god of righteousness. The ordeal procedure is very common in African society: Post, *Afrikanisch. Jurisprud.*, 2, p. 110.

154.1 *E.g.* the Eleusinian, Mithraic, and Phrygian Mysteries: for examples of it in savage initiation rites, see *Annual Report Smithsonian Institute*, 1899-1900, p. 435.

157.1 Sahagun, Jourdanet, pp. xxxix. and 455.

157.2 *Vide supra*, p. 57.

157.3 Vide *Archiv für Religionswissenschaft*, 1904, pp. 401-409.

158.1 Duchesne, *Origines du culte Chrétien*, transl. by M'Clure, p. 296.

159.1 Sahagun, *op. cit.*, pp. 340-341.

159.2 *Vide* Herzog, *Real-Encyclop., s.v. Beichte.*

160.1 King, *Babylonian Religion*, p. 212.

160.2 *Vide* Von der Goltz, *Das Gebet*, p. 297: Cabrol, *Prière Antique*, p. 316: the aspersion with holy water in the present Roman ritual does not seem to have been obligatory in the early period: *vide* Duchesne, *Origines*, p. 404, Engl. transl.

LECTURE IV NOTES

164.1 An interesting and original contribution to the solution of the question will be found in a recent paper by Mr R. Marett in *Folk-Lore*, 1904, "From Spell to Prayer."

166.1 *Vide* A. Lang, *The Making of Religion*.

167.1 Vide *Anthropolog. Journ.*, 1904, p. 165.

169.1 R. Marett, *op. cit.*, p. 145.

170.1 *Man*, 1902, p. 104.

170.2 Frazer, *Golden Bough* (2) iii. 83.

170.3 Plutarch, 693 F.

170.4 At the Anthesteria, Photius, *s.v.* Θύραζε κῆρες: Hesych., *s.v.*

171.1 Frazer, *op. cit.*, iii. 98: *vide* Marett, *op. cit.*, p. 163.

171.2 *Primitive Culture*, vol. ii. (concluding chapter).

175.1 Marett, *op. cit.*, p. 152.

176.1 Tylor, *op. cit.*, ii. p. 334.

176.2 Frazer, *Golden Bough,*(2) vol. ii. p. 212.

177.1 *Annual Report of Smithsonian Institute*, "Study of Sioux Cults, by Dorsey," 1899-1900, p. 381, etc.

178.1 *Peabody Museum Reports*, vol. iii. p. 276, etc.

178.2 *Annual Report Smithsonian Institute*, 1899-1900, pp. 420-421.

178.3 Tylor, *op. cit.*, ii. p. 331.

178.4 *Folk-Lore*, 1904, p. 168: *Toda Prayer*, W. H. R. Rivers.

179.1 Published by Carl Sapper in *Nördliches Mittel-Amerika*, vide *Archiv für vergl. Relig. Wiss.*, 1904, p. 468.

180.1 Budge, *Egyptian Magic*, p. 49.

180.2 Jastrow, *Religion Babyloniens Assyriens*, p. 490: *cf.* the formula in the prayer of one of the early kings to the goddess Ga-túm-dug: "I have no mother—Thou art my mother: I have no father—Thou art my father," Jastrow, p. 395.

180.3 *Sacred Books*, vol. xlvi. p. 23.

181.1 Vol. I.

183.1 Tylor, *Prim. Cult.*, ii. p. 333.

183.2 Tylor, *op. cit.*, ii. p. 335.

183.3 I have only space to make a summary reference here to the very noteworthy collection of Peruvian prayers preserved by De Molina, *Fables and Rites of the Yncas*, p. 28, etc., 38, 56: they have all the character of pure prayer, and occasionally reach a high spiritual level: the only appearance of magic is in the sacrifice that accompanies the singular petition "that the Creator and the sun may remain ever young."

184.1 *Vide* also Andrian in *Deutsch. Gesellsch. Anthropol.*, xxvii., 1896, p. 109.

185.1 Serv., *Æn.*, 2, 351.

185.2 *Fr. 781, Phaethon.*

185.3 *Vedic Hymns* (*Sacred Books*, etc.), pt. ii. p. 378.

187.1 l. 160: cf. *Plat. Crat.*, 400 E., "It is our custom in our prayers to call the gods by whatsoever name they most rejoice to be called by."

187.2 *Vedic Hymns*, pt. ii., pp. 281, 372.

188.1 Budge, *op. cit.*, p. 161.

188.2 Budge, *op. cit.*, pp. 137-141.

188.3 *Vide* examples quoted by Ausfeld, *De Græcorum Precationibus*, p. 519.

189.1 Ps. 54, 31.

189.2 c. 23, v. 21.

189.3 Joseph, *De bell. Jud.*, 2, 8.

189.4 Acts 8, 16; 19, 5.

190.1 Von der Goltz, *Das Gebet*, p. 353.

191.1 *Hymns of the Atharva-Veda* (*Sacred Books*, etc., xlii. p. 167).

191.2 *Vedic Hymns*, pt. ii. p. 391.

192.1 *Cf.* a formula in an Egyptian papyrus published by Kenyon (122, v. 13), "I know thee, Hermes, who thou art and whence thou art and what city is the city of Hermes": quoted by Ausfeld, *op. cit.* p. 524, *n.* 1.

193.1 The "Merseburg charm," old High German tenth-century MS.: *cf.* R. Chambers, *Fireside Stories*, Edinburgh, 1842. My attention was called to the great antiquity of this Norse charm by Prof. Napier, to whose kindness I owe these references.

193.2 *Sacred Books*, xlii. p. 20.

194.1 Golther, *op. cit.*, pp. 647-648.

194.2 In a pre-Conquest Cotton MS. in the British Museum, *vide* Grein's *Bibliothek der ängelsächsischen Poesie*: ed. Mülcker, vol. i. p. 316.

195.1 Livy, 22, 10.

196.1 De Re Rustica, 139, 141: Wordsworth, *Fragments and Specimens of Early Latin*, p. 335.

196.2 Clemens, *Strom.*, p. 754, Pott.

197.1 *Eumen.*, 332.

198.1 Dittenberger, *Sylloge*(2), vol. iii. 816.

198.2 Post, *Afrikanisch. Jurisprud.*, 2, p. 128.

199.1 Paus., 10, 12, 10.

200.1 πλεῖστον οὖλον ἵει, ἴουλον ἵει, Athenæ., 618 E.

200.2 The song sung by the children, probably an old weather-spell, called φιληλίας, with the refrain, ἔξεχ᾽ ὦ φίλ᾽ ἥλιε, Pollux, 9, 123, Athenæ., 619 B.

201.1 *Ephem. Archaiol.*, 1891, p. 82.

201.2 Plato, *Alcibiad.*, 2, p. 148 C.

202.1 Collitz, *Dialect-Inschrift.*, 1562, 1563, early fourth century B.C.

202.2 Collitz, 3648.

203.1 Roberts, *Greek Epigraphy*, vol. i. p. 304.

203.2 Nem., 8, 35.

203.3 Ol., 13, 115.

203.4 Med., 635.

203.5 Bergk, *Frag. Lyr. Græc.*, vol. iii., Scolia 2.

204.1 *Œcon.*, 11, 8.

204.2 *De Superst.*, p. 116 D.

204.3 Plat., *Phædr.*, 279 B.

204.4 Philostr., *Vit. Apoll.*, 4, 41.

205.1 Plat., *Alcib.*, 2, p. 143 A.

205.2 Epictet. (Schenkle), p. 479.

205.3 *Id.*, p. 158.

205.4 Von der Goltz, *Das Gebet*, p. 292.

206.1 Diog. Laert. 8, 16, 7: yet, according to Clemens, "The Pythagoreans enjoin that prayer should be uttered aloud, so that one might never pray for what one would be ashamed that others should hear," *Strom.*, p. 641, Pott.

206.2 Porphyry ap. Proclus *in Tim.*, 2, 64 B: Procl. *in Tim.*, 2, 65: Sallustius, *De Diis et Mundo*, c. 16: *cf.* Max. Tyr., *Dissert.* xi.

207.1 Vide *Archiv für vergl. Religionswissensch.*, 1904, p. 395.

207.2 The remarkable ethical fragment of an unknown philosopher, Eusebios, in Ionic dialect, quoted by Stobæus, περὶ ἀρετῆς, § 85 (vol. i. p. 39, Meineke), contains moral aspirations that strikingly resemble New Testament doctrine, and may possibly have been intended as a prayer, but it contains no appeal to a divinity: he may belong to the Neo-Platonic sect, *vide* Orelli, *Opusc. Græc. Sentent.*, vol. ii. p. 728.

208.1 *Vedic Hymns*, pt. ii. p. 61.

209.1 *E.g.*, "Protect our people all around with those undeceived guardians of thine, oh Agni," *ib.*, p. 158.

210.1 Atharva-Veda (*Sacred Books*, vol. xlii. p. 138).

210.2 *Vedic Hymns*, pt. ii. p. 376.

210.3 *Ib.*, p. 273.

210.4 *Ib.*, p. 383.

210.5 *Ib.*, p. 252.

211.1 Quoted by Prof. Tylor, *Primitive Culture*, vol. ii. p. 339, from Rig Veda, vii. 89, 3.

211.2 *Vedic Hymns*, pt. ii. p. 181.

211.3 *Ib.*, p. 249.

211.4 *Ib.*, p. 354.

211.5 Atharva-Veda, p. 164.

212.1 Atharva-Veda, p. 163.

212.2 *Ib.*, p. 165.

212.3 "Bring ye forward an ancient mighty speech to Agni.... May our prayers increase Agni," *Vedic Hymns*, pt. ii. p. 259: *cf.* p. 391, "The prayers fill thee (oh Agni) with power and strengthen thee, like great rivers the Sindhu."

214.1 *Sacred Books*, etc., vol. iv. (*Zend-Avesta*, pt. i. p. 228).

214.2 *Ib.*, pp. 145-147.

214.3 *Sacred Books*, etc., vol. xxxi. (*Zend-Avesta*, pt. iii. p. 262.)

215.1 *Zend-Avesta*, pt. i. p. 246.

215.2 *Cf.* the Greek sentiment, θυσία ἀρίστη γνώμη ἀγαθή, Joann. Damascen., *Sacr. Par.*, tit. ix. p. 640.

215.3 *Zend-Avesta*, pt. iii. p. 247.

216.1 *Zend-Avesta*, pt. i. p. 138.

217.1 Pt. i. p. 147.

217.2 Pt. iii. pp. 33-34.

217.3 *Ib.*, p. 179.

217.4 *Ib.*, p. 106.

217.5 *Ib.*, p. 49.

218.1 Pt. iii., p. 170.

218.2 *Archiv f. Religionswiss.*, 1904, p. 395.

218.3 Von der Goltz, *Das Gebet*, p. 288.

219.1 Jastrow, *Religion Babyloniens w. Assyriens*, vol. i. pp. 391-393, 423, 427.

219.2 *Ib.*, p. 497.

219.3 S. Aug., *De Civ. Dei.*, 10, 9.

220.1 King, *Babylonian Religion*, p. 83.

220.2 Jastrow, *op. cit.*, p. 401.

220.3 *Ib.*, p. 402.

221.1 Jastrow, *op. cit.*, p. 408.

221.2 *Ib.*, p. 411.

221.3 *Ib.*, p. 501: the elevated tone of the old Babylonian royal liturgy was still preserved under the later Seleukid rule, *vide* p. 414.

222.1 Jastrow, *op. cit.*, p. 501.

222.2 *Ib.*, p. 533.

222.3 *Ib.*, p. 536.

223.1 Jastrow, *op. cit.*, p. 509.

224.1 Jastrow, *op. cit.*, pp. 439-440.

225.1 Budge, *Egyptian Magic*, pp. 108, 110, 120.

225.2 *Ib.*, p. 127.

226.1 Budge, *Egyptian Magic*, p. 63.

226.2 *Ib.*, p. 119.

226.3 *Ib.*, p. 119.

227.1 Budge, *Egyptian Magic*, p. 184.

228.1 Origen, περὶ εὐχῆς, c. 10, 2.

228.2 Clemens, *Strom.*, vii., ch. 7, § 39, p. 854, Pott.

228.3 *Ib.*, § 38, p. 853, Pott.

229.1 *Vide* Von der Goltz, *op. cit.*, p. 310.

229.2 *Vide* Usener, *Archiv für Religionswiss.*, 1904, p. 293.

230.1 *Vide supra*, pp. 181-182.